THE HUMAN BRAIN

THE HUMAN BRAIN

···

A Guided Tour

SUSAN A. GREENFIELD

BasicBooks

A Division of HarperCollins*Publishers*

The Science Masters Series is a global publishing venture consisting of original science books written by leading scientists and published by a worldwide team of twenty-six publishers assembled by John Brockman. The series was conceived by Anthony Cheetham of Orion Publishers and John Brockman of Brockman Inc., a New York literary agency, and developed in coordination with BasicBooks.

• • • • • • • • • • •

The Science Masters name and marks are owned by and licensed to the publisher by Brockman Inc.

• • • • • • • • • • •

Published by BasicBooks,
A Division of HarperCollins Publishers, Inc.

• • • • • • • • • • •

FIRST EDITION

• • • • • • • • • • •

Library of Congress Cataloging-in-Publication Data

Greenfield, Susan
    The human brain : a guided tour / by Susan A. Greenfield.
        p. cm. — (Science master series)
    Includes index.
    ISBN 0-465-00725-2
    1. Brain—Popular works. I. Title. II. Series.
    QP376.G695   1997
    612.8'2—DC21   97-5131
                                                        CIP

97 98 99 00 01 ❖/RRD 10 9 8 7 6 5 4 3 2 1

To Doris and Reg Greenfield

CONTENTS

ACKNOWLEDGMENTS

I would like to thank the following colleagues at the University of Oxford, for making helpful suggestions to the manuscript: Dr. O. Paulsen (Dept. of Pharmacology), Dr. J. Taylor (Dept. of Human Anatomy), Professor J. Stein (Dept. of Physiology), and Professor A. D. Smith (Dept. of Pharmacology). I am also extremely grateful for my editors at HarperCollins, Susan Rabiner and Patricia Bozza, and above all, to my husband, Peter, for his constant support.

Many people are intrigued by the brain. However, they have no immediate means of discovering even the most basic and well-established facts. Only technical books are currently available, more appropriate to students in the biomedical sciences with the necessary background knowledge: the average person would be, and is, readily discouraged by the plethora of specialist terminology. At the same time, the brain holds an urgent fascination for virtually everyone since it encompasses a wide range of issues, at least one of which has interested each of us personally: for example, infant development, use and abuse of drugs, strokes, schizophrenia, brain scans, or the physical basis of consciousness.

I have written this book to introduce not just nonbiologists but nonstudents to what lies within their skull. My aim is to show people what we already know about the brain and mind, and what questions we can realistically answer with our current expertise. Although I had long contemplated such a book, two experiences finally jolted me into action. In 1994 I was asked to give the Royal Institution Christmas Lectures for that year. These lectures, on a wide range of scientific subjects, have been enthralling audiences of young people since 1826, and for the last thirty or so years they have been televised by the British Broadcasting Corporation (BBC). The programs are an established part of British life not least because they are so different from conventional lectures: since the time of the founding speaker, Michael Faraday, there has been an emphasis on live demonstrations involving audience participation, working models, antique props, and all varieties of exotic animals.

The five chapters in this book have been very broadly inspired by each of the five lectures. However, although I have endeavored to incorporate some of the spirit, and indeed material, of the Christmas Lectures, there are some very basic differences. Whereas the lectures were aimed at an audience of teenagers, I have directed this book to an adult readership. Moreover, the impact of a live eagle and owl, or the amusement of a reaction-times contest, does not translate effectively to the printed page. I have therefore put far less emphasis here on giving a wide range of examples of phenomena and principles, and have turned my attention to the more "philosophical" implications of studying the brain. In short, I have taken the liberty of indulging in all manner of speculations as to how the "mind" might arise from the brain. These ideas are not intended to be taken as hard facts but rather to excite readers into an active line of questioning and thought of their own.

This approach has been nurtured further by the second opportunity I have had to talk about the brain to the general public. In 1995 I was elected to the Chair of Physics at Gresham College, London. In accordance with the will of an Elizabethan financier, Thomas Gresham, the eight professors representing each branch of what was then perceived as the "new learning" were obliged to lecture to the public free of charge within the City of London. Accordingly, I have been giving introductory lectures on the brain for the last two years in a style which, I hope, is comprehensible to everyone who walks through the door, even if they are attending the lectures for the first time. I have thus had a marvelous chance to observe firsthand the kind of questions people ask and to appreciate the particular subjects that interest them. These experiences have contributed a great deal to helping me with the selection of material and its presentation.

In Chapter 1 we survey the brain with nothing but the naked eye and explore the relevance of different brain regions. Does each have a different function? In Chapter 2 the problems of localization of brain functions are approached by examining certain familiar functions such as movement and vision, and attempting to see how they are accommodated in the brain. In Chapter 3 the emphasis shifts from gross brain regions to the brain under a microscope. We see how the basic building blocks of the brain—brain cells—communicate with each other, and how such communication can be modified by drugs. In Chapter 4 we trace how a brain is made from a single fertilized egg. The fate of the brain is followed through life as we see how it constantly changes as a result of experience to provide the essence of a unique individual. In the fifth chapter we follow up this idea of individuality by asking what memory is, how it works, and where it occurs in the brain. It is through memory that we finally have a glimpse of the physical basis for the mind.

The brain still remains a tantalizing mystery: to those of us who have been studying it for most of our lives it often seems that the more we learn, the more there is still to learn. It is a little like the monster of Greek mythology, the hydra: once one head was cut off, seven grew in its place. This book offers no magic bullets to the secret of individuality or consciousness, nor does it promise easy answers. However, it will, I hope, help foster curiosity and appreciation of the most exciting entity in the universe.

THE HUMAN BRAIN

···

CHAPTER I

BRAINS WITHIN BRAINS

How does the brain work? What does it actually do? These questions have fascinated and challenged countless human beings over many centuries. At last, however, we now have the expertise to tackle what might arguably be regarded as the final frontier in human understanding. We also have the motivation.

People are living longer, but not necessarily better. The devastating illnesses of old age that attack the brain, such as Parkinson's and Alzheimer's diseases, are becoming more prevalent. Moreover, the pressures of modern life have led to a huge increase in psychiatric illnesses such as depression and anxiety. In addition, there is a growing dependence on mood-modifying drugs. Therefore, we are faced with an urgent need to understand as much as we can about the brain. On July 17, 1990, the then president of the United States, George Bush, proclaimed that every effort should be made to "enhance public awareness of the benefits to be derived from brain research." We are currently in the middle of the "Decade of the Brain." A general interest in the brain is official.

Remote from the rest of the body in its own custom-built casing of skull bone, the brain has a consistency similar to a soft-boiled egg and has no intrinsic moving parts. Thus, it is obviously not destined to take any physical strain or participate in any large-scale mechanical actions. The Greeks came to the conclusion that this insubstantial and secretive substance was the perfect site for the soul. Most importantly, soul was immortal: it had nothing to do with thinking. In fact, all the abilities we now attribute to the brain, the Greeks localized in the heart or the lungs (there was never total agreement about the precise location). The immortal "soul" was of course so sacred and elusive that the silent, remote gray home provided for it by the brain presented a serious focus with almost mystical properties: the Greeks imposed strict taboos against eating the brains of any animal. The soul in this case was quite explicitly a different entity from "consciousness" and the "mind" and all the other interesting properties that we now associate with our individuality and personality.

Such quirky reasoning, where normal mental activities were not associated at all with the brain, changed with a great discovery made by Alcmaeon of Croton. Alcmaeon showed that there were actual connections leading from the eyes to the brain. Surely, he claimed, this area must be the seat of thought. This revolutionary idea tied in with observations made by two Egyptian anatomists, Herophilus and Erasistratus, who managed to trace nerves—obviously not identified as such at the time—leading from the rest of the body into the brain. But if the brain was the center for thinking, what about the soul?

The Greek physician Galen (A.D. 129–199) pointed to a part of the brain that was the least solid, the most ethereal, and clearly discernible to the naked eye. Deep within the brain is a labyrinth of interconnecting cavities, formed during development in the womb and containing a colorless fluid. This insubstantial-seeming fluid bathes the whole of the outer surface of the brain and spinal cord and is known as cerebrospinal fluid (CSF). It is often used in the diagnosis of various neurological problems when sampled from the lower portion of the spinal cord in a lumbar puncture. Normally, however, the CSF is reabsorbed into the blood supply, so that fresh fluid is constantly being produced (about 0.2 milliliters per minute in humans) and is thus constantly circulating.

It is easy to imagine how this mysterious swirling substance, as opposed to the sluggish slurry of brain, might have been a good candidate for the substance of the soul. We now know that the CSF contains merely salts, sugars, and certain proteins. Far from being the seat of the soul, it has even been disparagingly referred to as "the urine of the brain." No one, even those who believe in an immortal soul, now expects to find it in the brain. The mortal brain, which everyone regards as obviously responsible for all our thoughts and feelings, presents in itself the most tantalizing of riddles.

In this book we are going to see how far we can progress with answering the question: How does the brain work? But this question is far too global and vague to have any meaning in terms of actual experiments or observations. What we need to do instead is to tackle more specific subquestions that nonetheless make a contribution to a final understanding of this secretive mass of tissue in which, somehow, the essence of our personalities is locked away.

The first topic we shall explore in this chapter is the physical appearance of the brain. Imagine you were looking at a brain in your hands: what you would be holding would be a creamy colored, wrinkled object weighing just over 1 kilogram, on average about 1.3 kilograms. (See Figure 1.) The first feature you would notice is that the strange-looking object, small enough to be supported in one cupped palm, is made up of distinct regions of a particular shape and texture that fold around each other and interlock according to some grand scheme that we are only now beginning to discern.

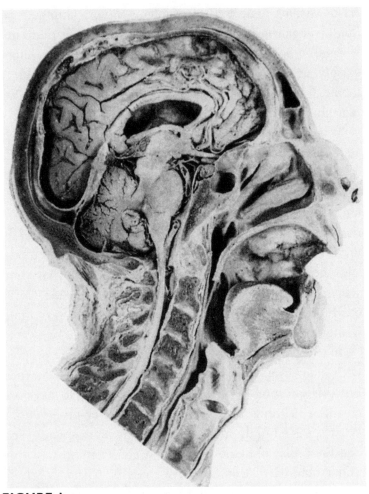

FIGURE I

A cross-section of the human brain within the head. Note how the brain is composed of different gross regions easily discernible to the naked eye, and how it is continuous with the spinal cord.

[From *A Colour Atlas of the Brain and Spinal Cord* by M. A. England and J. Wakely (London: Wolfe Publishing Ltd., 1991)]

The brain has the consistency of a raw egg with an overall ground plan that is always the same. There are two clear halves, called hemispheres, that seem to sit around a kind of thick stalk (brain stem). This brain stem eventually tapers down into the spinal cord. At the back is a cauliflower-shaped extrusion, a "little brain" (cerebellum) that protrudes precariously behind the main brain (cerebrum).

If you were to look at the cerebellum, the brain stem, and the surface of these hemispheres, you would see that they are all different in surface texture, as well as varying slightly in color along the cream–pink-brown spectrum. Furthermore, if you turned the brain over and looked at the underside, it would be easy to see still further different regions again distinguishable by color, texture, and shape. For the most part, each region is duplicated on either side of the brain so that you could draw a line down the middle as an axis, about which the brain would be symmetrical.

The different regions of the brain pile around the stalk-like brain stem and are divided up by neuroscientists in an ordered anatomical scheme. One way to think of these brain regions is as countries distinguished by boundaries. Often these boundaries are very obvious: one might be a fluid-filled ventricle where we saw the soul was once thought to lurk, another might be subtly changed in texture or color. According to the recognized scheme, each region has a different name, but we will be gathering such labels (for example, cerebellum or brain stem) only as we need them. Rather than a detailed documentation of the anatomy of the brain, our prime concern here is to discover how certain regions contribute to the feats of survival in the outside world as well as to consciousness of that inner world, one's most private place of thoughts and feelings. These issues have tantalized people since long before the dawning of the Decade of the Brain.

For some, such as Marcello Malpighi in the seventeenth century, the brain functioned homogeneously, as a huge gland. Malpighi's vision was that the nervous system was like an inverted tree. The trunk was in the spinal cord, with the roots in the brain and the branches in the nerves extending throughout the body. A little later, in the first part of the eighteenth century, Jean-Pierre-Marie Flourens also concluded that the brain was homogeneous, from the results of his rather ghoulish experiments. Flourens employed a very simple rationale: to remove different parts of the brain and see what functions remained. He experimented on a variety of laboratory animals, methodically removing more and more of their brains and observing the effects. What he found was that all functions grew progressively weaker, rather than selective functions becoming specifically impaired. With undeniable logic, Flourens decided that distinct functions could not be localized as such within selective parts of the brain.

This scenario of a uniform brain with no specialist parts inspired the concept of mass action. It is an idea that still persists today, in a less extreme form, in order to explain a seeming miraculous but fairly frequent occurrence: when parts of the brain are destroyed, say by stroke, then after a while other intact parts appear to take over, so that at least some of the original function is restored.

In complete contrast to this idea is the view that the brain can be divided into rigid compartments, each with a highly specific function. The most famous proponent of this vision was Franz Gall, a doctor born in Vienna in 1758. Gall was very interested in the human mind, but he considered it too delicate to probe surgically. Given the techniques of the time, he was probably quite right. Instead, Gall hit upon another, seemingly more subtle way of studying the brain. He developed the theory that if he studied the skulls of the dead and then saw how these matched up with the alleged characters of those people, then perhaps he could identify a physical trait that corresponded with certain aspects of character. The aspects of the brain that Gall chose to match up were the most easy feature to detect: the bumps on the surface of the skull.

Gall concluded that there were twenty-seven different character traits. These purported building blocks of personality actually turned out to be rather sophisticated features of the human mind: instinct of reproduction, love for one's offspring, attachment and friendship, defensive instinct of oneself and one's property, instinct for cruelty, cleverness, feeling of possessiveness and inclination to steal, pride and love of authority, vanity, circumspection and foresight, memory of things and facts, sense of spatial relations, memory for people, sense of words, sense of the spoken word, sense of color, sense of tonal relations, sense of the relationship of numbers, sense of mechanics, comparative wisdom, depth of thought and metaphysical spirit, sense of humor and sarcasm, poetic talent, goodness, faculty of imitating, God and religion, steadfastness.

With these different qualities—which were eventually expanded to thirty-two to include, for example, banality—a map of the surface of the head was produced, where the functions were localized to greater or lesser degrees, according to whether the lumps were small or large in each individual. The nagging and still unanswerable question was not even raised of how a specific mental state might ever be associated with a physical infrastructure, let alone one as remote from brain tissue as a bump on the skull.

The apparatus that Gall used to make his analyses was a kind of hat. When placed on the skull, movable pins were displaced by the bumps on the surface of the skull so that they were pushed upward to pierce through paper. The particular pattern of perforations in the paper thus gave a somewhat primitive readout of an individual's character. Johann Caspar Spurzheim, one of Gall's colleagues, coined the Greek term *phrenology*, "the study of the mind," to describe the procedure and its underlying philosophy. It offered a new way of looking at the brain, and because it relied on objective measurements, it had all the luster of a true science—as such it rapidly captured the spirit of the times. Phrenology became popular because it seemed to present people with a more "scientific" approach as well as with a new basis for morality, something that could be measured and did not entail difficult and abstract ideas, like soul. Seen as a secular, objective system, stripped of any need for blind faith, phrenology catered superbly to the growing number of people disaffected at that time with the church.

Another advantage was, of course, that it was a new way of making large amounts of money: phrenology pamphlets, books, and models all started to proliferate. Indeed phrenology became an integral part of many people's lives. Just as today items ranging from mugs to jewelry bear signs of the zodiac, so in the last century walking canes, for example, would have a tiny, personalized phrenology bust on the handle. But eventually this fascinating, painless, and lucrative endeavor was to run into trouble.

In 1861, in France, the neuroanatomist and anthropologist Paul Broca examined a man who was unable to speak. This man could only say "tan": he couldn't pronounce any other words, hence he was referred to as "Tan," even though his real name was Leborgne. Tan earned his place in history because six days after the examination he had the misfortune to die, thereby giving Broca the chance to examine his brain. It turned out that the area of the brain damaged was completely different from that predicted by phrenology. On some phrenology busts, the center for language is localized in the lower part of the left eye socket, whereas in Tan's brain, the damaged area was a small region toward the front of the left-hand side of the brain. Henceforth this part of the brain became known as *Broca's area.*

Because it did not match up with unequivocal clinical observations such as these, phrenology started to lose its appeal. The problem was compounded when, a few years later, another physician, the Austrian Carl Wernicke, discovered a different type of speech problem. In the patients that Wernicke studied, there was damage to a completely different part of the brain. In this case the patient, unlike Tan, could articulate words perfectly. The only problem in

Wernicke's aphasia is that the speech is often gibberish. Words are jumbled together in an incoherent sequence and frequently new words are invented with no apparent meaning at all.

The discovery of yet another area of the brain, clearly associated with, but linked to a different aspect of, speech, shows that the problem for phrenology was not even a mislocation of the speech center: Wernicke's observations raised the even deeper issue that, irrespective of location, even the concept of a single speech center is not valid. Bumps on the skull clearly do not represent different brain functions. Irrespective of the absurdity of measuring bumps on the skull as an index of brain function, there is still the problem of how a cohesive behavior, skill, sensation, or thought is translated into a physical event somewhere in the brain, and vice versa. The phrenologists thought that there was a simple one-to-one mapping of the complete finished product—a complex function such as language—with a single, small region. In retrospect it is easy to see that they were wrong, although the idea of centers of memory, emotion, and so forth still persists in folklore views of the brain. But if chunks of the brain are not merely passively and directly corresponding to chunks of the outside world, or chunks of our behavioral and mental repertoire, then what kind of alternative scenario can be envisaged?

John Hughlings-Jackson (1835–1911), a British neurologist, viewed the brain as organized into a hierarchy. The most primitive drives were kept in check by higher restraining functions that were increasingly more sophisticated, and hence most developed in humans. This idea was to have implications for neurology, psychiatry, and even sociology. Abnormal movements resulting from brain damage could now be interpreted as an unleashing of lower functions, involuntary movements from their normal restraining higher influences. Similarly, Sigmund Freud was able to refer to the passionate drives of the "id" as being restrained by the "ego" (consciousness), which was kept in check by the conscience of the "superego." Finally, even in the political arena, far beyond an individual brain, the anarchic behavior of an ungoverned mob could also be interpreted as having escaped from a "higher" controlling force.

Although Hughlings-Jackson's idea is appealing in that it provides an interesting common framework for neurology, psychiatry, and even crowd behavior, the erroneous assumption made by the phrenologists lurks here also. The concept of a hierarchy implies something must be at the top, that there must be some ultimate controller. However, the idea of a single executive center for memory or movement is redolent of the bumps on a phrenology bust. Alternatively, the idea of an ultimate superego, while understandable in psychiatric or moral terms, does not have a physical counterpart as such. There is no mini–super brain within the brain directing all operations.

Another attempt at a scheme for interrelating the functioning of gross brain regions to each other was developed by Paul Maclean in the 1940s and 1950s. Again, Maclean viewed the brain as a kind of hierarchy, but this time composed of three tiers: the most "primitive reptilian," the more advanced "old mammalian," and the most sophisticated "new mammalian." The reptilian brain, which corresponded to the brain stem (the central stalk arising from the spinal cord), was responsible for instinctive behavior. By contrast, the old mammalian brain was constituted from a series of interconnecting middle brain–level structures known as the limbic system, which controlled emotional behavior, particularly aggression and sex. Finally, the new mammalian brain was the area for rational thought processes housed in the outer layer of the brain. This outer region is known as the *cortex,* derived from the Latin for "bark," since it covers the outer surface of the brain as does the bark on a tree.

Maclean referred to his concept as the *triune brain* and maintained that much of the conflict arising from the human condition resulted from a poor coordination between the three tiers. Although this theory might help us understand the literally mindless and uniform behavior of masses at political rallies, it does little to throw light on the central topic of this chapter: how functions in the outside world are actually localized in the brain.

Nonetheless, a comparison of the brains of the different species, such as reptiles, nonhuman mammals, and humans, might provide some clues to the puzzle. In the brains from different animals, the most obvious feature is that they vary in size. An easy deduction then is that the size of the brain is all important, that the bigger the brain the more intelligent the animal.

An elephant's brain is five times bigger than a human brain: it weighs about 8 kilograms, but would we say that an elephant is five times more intelligent than a person? Presumably not; some people claim that since elephants are a lot bigger than humans, it might not be size that is important on its own but rather the percentage of body weight that is made up of brain. The elephant brain is only 0.2 percent of its body weight compared to the human brain, which is 2.33 percent of body weight.

But percentage of body weight is not the entire story: the shrew's brain is about 3.33 percent of its body weight yet no one would claim that the shrew is particularly intelligent—in fact, the shrew is not at all famous for what it thinks. Perhaps the most celebrated fact about this little creature is what it needs to eat, namely its own body weight of insects every day. Therefore, other than size and ratio to body weight, there must be other critical facts about the brain.

So far we have been considering only absolute brain size, treating the brain as a single homogeneous mass, but remember the critical and basic feature of the brain is that it is composed of different regions. If we are exploring the significance of different brain regions, it might be very helpful to turn once more to evolution and see how individual human brain regions compare with those of other animals.

In species as different as a reptile such as the crocodile and a bird such as the cockerel, a basic and consistent format for the brain nonetheless starts to emerge. Some regions have hardly changed at all over time: for example, the stalk that rises from the spinal cord, the brain stem, is recognizable as a landmark in most cases. However, there are variations on a theme: for example, in the cockerel, the cerebellum, the "little brain," is about half of the total brain mass. In contrast, in certain fish the cerebellum can actually reach up to 90 percent of the total mass of the brain. The cerebellum must have a function that is common in the behavior of a wide range of animals, including humans, but is nonetheless particularly dominant in the repertoire of cockerels, and even more important still in fish.

For animals such as humans, with more sophisticated lifestyles, the cerebellum constitutes a far smaller fraction of the total brain. It seems reasonable to presume that the cerebellum is not linked closely to the more varied and idiosyncratic repertoire of behavior of which we are capable and for which we must presumably have more complicated brains. In contrast to the cerebellum, the brain region that has undergone the most change during evolution is the outer layer of the brain, the cortex.

An important clue to brain function is that in more sophisticated animals the cortex is folded—convoluted—so that its surface area has been able to increase while respecting the confines of a relatively small skull. Flattened out, the rat cortex would be the size of a postage stamp, that of the chimp would be the size of a piece of standard typing paper, while the human brain would be four times greater still! Humans have the least stereotyped, most flexible lifestyle of all animal species, and it is believed the cortex must therefore in some way be related to liberating the individual from fixed, predetermined patterns of behavior. The more extensive the cortex, the more an individual will be able to react in a specific, unpredictable fashion in accordance with the dictates of a complex situation. The more extensive the cortex, the more an animal will be able to think for itself. But what is really meant by the term *thinking?*

The cortex is about 2 millimeters thick and can be divided, according to different conventions, into functions that each belong to fifty to a hundred completely separate areas. Up to a point this type of classification makes sense: certain areas of the cortex, but by no means all, seem to have a clear correspondence with brain inputs and outputs. For example, the brain sends signals from nerves from a highly localized part of the cortex down through the spinal cord to contract muscles—hence this region of cortex is known as the motor cortex. At the same time there are other specific areas of the cortex—for example, the visual cortex and auditory cortex—that receive and process signals from the eyes and ears respectively. In a similar fashion, nerves in the skin carrying signals relating to pain and touch are sent up the spinal cord to the area of the cortex that responds to incoming signals regarding touch, the somatosensory cortex.

However, there are other regions of the cortex that cannot be so neatly classified. For example, a region toward the back of the head at the top (posterior parietal cortex) receives input from the visual, auditory, and somatosensory systems. Thus, the function of such a region is less obvious. Patients with damage to the parietal cortex display a wide range of impairments, according to the exact area and extent of the lesion. These symptoms can include a failure to recognize objects by sight or touch, or a failure to recognize with one sense what has already been experienced with another: for example, someone with parietal lobe damage might be unable to recognize by sight a ball that he or she had previously held while blindfolded. As well as these disorders with the senses, the output of the brain, the motor system, is also disturbed. For example, parietal patients can be clumsy (apraxia) in manipulating objects or even dressing. They can confuse left and right and have disorders of spatial skills. As well as these problems involving the main sensory inputs and motor outputs of the brain, damage to the parietal lobe can result in some very bizarre thinking. For example, patients may deny that half of their body actually belongs to them. This phenomenon is part of a still wider problem where they neglect all tactile, visual, and auditory stimulation of that side of the body.

It is important to realize that patients with damage to their parietal lobes have fully operational sensory systems and can move their muscles perfectly well. Rather, the problem appears to lie in the massive coordination of senses and movement that we normally take for granted. Because it seems that in some way the parietal cortex relates one sensory system to another, or indeed sensory systems to motor systems, this cortical region has become known as the *association cortex*. But a cortical area such as the parietal cortex does not just act as a simple crossroads for the inputs and outputs of the brain. In addition, there are problems of recognition for parietal patients, possibly leading to bizarre denials of half their body: in turn, this "neglect" can give rise to even wilder claims that their arm, for example, belongs to someone else. Clearly then, the parietal cortex, like other "association" areas of cortex, must be responsible for the most sophisticated and elusive functions of all: thinking, or as neuroscientists prefer, *cognitive processes*.

Returning to the strategy of comparing specific brain regions in different species, we might expect that cortical association areas were most marked in animals with the most sophisticated, individualistic lifestyles. Even compared to our nearest relative, the chimpanzee, with whom our deoxyribonucleic acid (DNA) differs by only 1 percent, the areas of association cortex are indeed several times greater. It is not surprising that it is these areas of cortex not directly allocated to controlling movement or to processing our senses that are the most intriguing, and at the same time the hardest to understand in terms of exactly what they do and how they do it.

For example, a large part of association cortex (see Figure 2) is found at the front of the brain, the prefrontal cortex. Of all the regions of cortex, this region has demonstrated the most spectacular growth: during mammalian evolution it

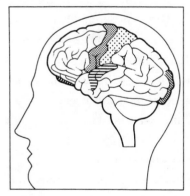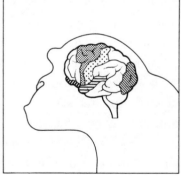

FIGURE 2

Comparison of the cortex of the chimpanzee and human. Note that more of the cortex of the chimpanzee is devoted to specific functions (shaded areas), whereas the human has many more parts of the cortex that are not allocated to clear roles (unshaded areas)—association cortex—particularly in the front of the brain (prefrontal cortex).

[Adapted from P. Corsi (ed.), *The Enchanted Loom*]

has increased 3 percent in cats, 17 percent in chimps, and a staggering 29 percent in humans. The first clue as to the actual function of the prefrontal cortex is from a chance event that happened in 1848 in Vermont.

At that time in the United States there was an enormous expansion of the railways. Phineas Gage was a foreman on a railway gang and it was his job to push dynamite down a hole in order to explode any obstacles that blocked the passage where the track was going to be laid. In order to apply the dynamite, Phineas had to use a rodlike object known as a tamping iron, which in this case was 3 feet 7 inches long, and at its widest point was 1.25 inches across.

One day Phineas was pushing dynamite down the hole with his tamping iron, when a tragic accident happened. By chance, a spark ignited the dynamite prematurely and it exploded. Although there was a very hefty explosion, Phineas survived, but not without some injury. He had been holding his head to one side, such that the premature ignition of the dynamite drove the tamping iron up through the left-hand side of his skull. The iron went through the bone into the front of the brain, severely damaging his prefrontal cortex. Amazingly, after a brief period of unconsciousness, Phineas seemed to be remarkably unaffected by such a dramatic course of events. Once the infection had cleared up, his senses and movements were as though nothing had ever happened.

But as time went on people started to notice a difference. Whereas before he had been a cooperative and friendly person, Phineas now became overbearing, indecisive, arrogant, obstinate, and uncaring for others. In fact, he eventually left his job on the railway and ended up living the rest of his life as a fairground freak, touring with the tamping iron still lodged in his brain.

After this incident, more startling cases of brain damage were reported, all more or less indicating the same idea: the prefrontal cortex does not appear to be related to brute survival skills such as breathing or regulating temperature, or to the processing of any of the senses or the coordination of movement, but rather with the most sophisticated aspects of our mind, the essence of our personality and how we react as individuals to the world. Such anecdotes are immediately interesting because in retrospect they reveal that our characters, which we think of as fairly fixed and inviolate aspects of ourselves, are really at the mercy of our physical brain: they *are* our brain. For current purposes they also raise less philosophical, more specific questions regarding the function of the area of brain in question, the prefrontal cortex. Is this single area that controls character a kind of executive minibrain within a brain? Such a concept was even too gross for phrenologists who devised subdivisions of character and erroneously distributed them in different regions. What then is the function of this frontal brain area?

In 1935, a Portuguese neurologist, Egas Moniz, attended the Second International Congress in London. It was at this meeting that he heard a report of an apparently neurotic monkey who became much more relaxed after its frontal lobes were lesioned. Inspired, Moniz proposed a similar approach to treating difficult humans. He developed the technique of *leucotomy,* from the Greek for "cutting the white (nerve fibers)" that connected the frontal lobes to the rest of the brain. Until the 1960s, frontal leucotomies were the treatment of choice for a whole range of very intense and persistent emotional responses such as depression, anxiety, phobias, and aggression. Between 1936 and 1978, some 35,000 people in the United States underwent the surgical procedure. In order to appreciate just how many individuals were so treated, take a look at everyone listed as "Smith" in the New York City telephone directory! Since the late 1960s there has been a decline in the number of leucotomies performed each year. The development of more sophisticated drugs as well as a final realization of the cognitive deficits that can result from the surgery have stayed the hands of clinicians for whom surgery would have seemed the only possible course of action a few decades earlier.

During their heydey, leucotomies were claimed to result in few side effects. It gradually became apparent, however, that there was no net arguable therapeutic benefit and indeed that the side effects were severe. As with Phineas, these patients became changed characters, lacking in foresight and emotionally unresponsive. In line with this apparent inability to be proactive, patients with damaged frontal lobes are less able to develop novel strategies or plans to tackle a particular problem. They cannot use information from their environment to regulate or change behavior; instead, they perseverate.

This profile of dysfunction has been characterized by studying the performance on certain specific experimental tasks of patients and indeed monkeys who have damage in the frontal lobes. For example, such subjects cannot switch rules if they are doing something, such as sorting cards according to color of symbols, when subsequently asked to sort according to shape of symbol. Some people refer to this ability, which we all normally have, as working memory, a working framework in which a task is performed and which is sometimes dubbed the "blackboard of the mind." With failures in working memory, it is hard to remember events in a proper context. But the problem of damage to the prefrontal cortex is not just one of memory. Another result of this damage is loss of verbal spontaneity: patients with damage to the prefrontal cortex tend to volunteer less information, as well as displaying the impaired social behavior that we saw with Phineas.

Despite this wealth of information, it is still hard to say exactly what might be the function of the prefrontal lobes. Some neuroscientists have pointed to the similarities between patients with prefrontal lobe damage and schizophrenia. Schizophrenics also appear to have problems on the same working memory tasks as the neurological patients. Hence schizophrenia has been interpreted as a disorder of matching up incoming information with internalized standards, rules, or expectations. The schizophrenic and prefrontal patient would both be overwhelmed and dominated by a sensory input that they could not adequately categorize or by memories that they could not fit into the correct temporal sequence. It is almost as though they lack the inner resources that act for most of us as shock absorbers to the happenstance of life. However, if such a hypothesis is true, it is too complex and abstract a process, with far too many different aspects, consequences, and corollaries, to be summed up as a single and identifiable function in our daily lives. If we were phrenologists, it would be hard to think of a one-word label that could be appropriately placed on the frontal lobes.

We can say that a patient has social problems or problems with working memory, but it is very hard to find out what the common factor is between these two disparate impairments. Indeed for many, if not most, areas of the brain, it is hard to match up familiar events in the outside world exclusively with actual events in a single brain region. Different parts of the cortex, such as the motor cortex and the somatosensory cortex, clearly have different functions, and association areas such as the prefrontal cortex and parts of the parietal cortex must each have their own type of specialized roles. But contrary to the phrenologists' vision, these roles do not correspond on a one-to-one basis with obvious aspects of our character and specific activities in the real world. It is one of the biggest challenges in neuroscience today to understand the relationship between what is actually going on within certain brain regions and how such internalized physiological events are reflected in outward behavior.

The cases of Phineas Gage and leucotomized patients

illustrate one approach used in brain study by those trying to identify the role of a specific brain region: look at examples of damage to a particular brain region and infer its erstwhile function from whatever dysfunction is now apparent. One well-known example of selective brain damage that might have been thought to indicate immediately and directly the function of the area in question is Parkinson's disease.

Parkinson's disease was originally named after James Parkinson, who first reported the condition in 1817. This severe disorder of movement affects mainly older people, although younger people can sometimes fall victim. Patients have great difficulty in moving; in addition, they might have a tremor when their hands are at rest and stiffness of their limbs. The fascinating aspect of Parkinson's disease is that unlike many disorders of the brain, such as depression or schizophrenia, we know exactly where the problem lies, in an area deep down in the middle of the brain.

At the very core of this middle part of the brain lies a moustache-shaped, black-colored area consequently named in Latin *substantia nigra* (black mass). The substantia nigra appears black because the cells in this region have the pigment melanin in them. Melanin is in turn the end product of an important brain chemical, dopamine, after it has undergone various chemical reactions. Hence it is now firmly established that cells in the substantia nigra are normally making the chemical dopamine.

Similarly, it has been known for a long time that if a normal brain is compared with a Parkinsonian one, then the substantia nigra in the brain of a patient with Parkinson's disease is much paler—the cells containing the pigment have died. One of the important consequences of these cells dying is that the chemical dopamine is no longer being manufactured in this region. If Parkinsonian patients are given a tablet of the chemical (L-DOPA) from which dopamine is made, then there is a dramatic improvement in movement. Even though we know exactly where the damage is in Parkinson's disease—that is, the substantia nigra—and even though we know what particular chemical is deficient—that is, dopamine—no one has any precise idea as to the function of the substantia nigra in normal movement.

Moreover, we cannot ignore the fact that Parkinson's disease involves not just the substantia nigra as an anatomical region but is also specific to the chemical dopamine. Some might view the substantia nigra as the mere location from which the critical cells deliver dopamine to another more relevant target brain region, the striatum. The important question would then be: What is the function of dopamine in the striatum? The anatomy of the brain does not directly match up with the chemistry of the brain: there is no one chemical exclusive to any one brain region. Rather, the same chemical is distributed over many different brain regions while each brain region makes and uses many different brain chemicals. It is therefore very hard to say what is most important when considering brain damage—the brain region concerned or the change in the chemical balance in the brain.

There is another reason for being wary when trying to pin down particular functions to particular brain areas: neuronal plasticity. Brain areas can, of course, be damaged for many reasons whether it be disease, car accident, or gunshot, but a very common reason is stroke. A stroke occurs when there is not enough oxygen in the brain. This lack of oxygen could be due to a blood vessel that has become blocked, thus preventing access of the blood normally carrying oxygen around the brain, or because there is a reduction in blood flow due to a narrowing of the blood vessels. If a stroke occurs, in the motor cortex for example, then it is possible to trace a sequence of rather interesting events that unfold.

Initially after such a stroke there may be no movement at all, not even reflexes: the limb on the affected side of the body just dangles loosely (flaccid paralysis). Then a seeming miracle occurs over a period of days and weeks, although the extent of the miracle will vary enormously from patient to patient. First of all, reflexes can return, then the arm will start to be rigid and the patient will be able to make limb movements, and finally the stroke victim will be able to grasp something. In one study, a third of the patients who had stroke in the motor cortex were able to grasp objects spontaneously and hence reach this final stage of recovery.

There are also reports of recovery from brain damage that have affected speech and memory after certain head injuries. Brain functions therefore need not belong to one area, to one particular population of neurons—how otherwise could recovery of function occur if the original cells in question, with their exclusive monopoly, were dead? Instead, it is as though other brain cells were gradually learning to take over the role of the damaged cells. Indeed, the stages of recovery of the grasping movement that we have just traced following stroke in the motor cortex are very similar to the initial development of this same movement in infants, as we shall see in Chapter 4. Again, it is hard to claim that one part of the brain definitely does one thing; if other, albeit adjacent, brain areas can take over that role, then clearly there is at least a degree of flexibility, known as neuronal plasticity.

How then might we study the function of different brain regions? What we really need is a snapshot, or better still a video, of the inside of the brain as a person is thinking, talking, or performing any of a variety of usual functions. The story of how this ideal is actually becoming a reality starts with a familiar procedure: the use of X rays. X rays are high-frequency, short-duration electromagnetic waves. Because X-ray radiation is very high energy, it readily penetrates a test object: the atoms in this test object absorb some of the radiation, leaving the unabsorbed portion to strike a photographic plate, thereby exposing it. Thus, the less radiodense an object, the darker the photographic plate, whereas the more radiodense an object, the whiter the photographic plate. This process, as we all know, works very well at security checks in airports for material where there is great contrast, such as a gun inside a suitcase, or in hospitals to visualize broken bones in flesh.

Although X rays are effective for detecting what is happening in most of the body, when it comes to the brain there is a problem. Unlike the contrast between bone and flesh, there is little difference in the density of one brain region compared to another. To overcome this hurdle, a solution would be to make the brain more radiopaque, or alternatively to make the technique of X rays more sensitive.

Let's look first at how the inside of the brain itself could be made to resemble the scenario of the gun in a case, how certain components could be made to give greater contrast compared with the rest of the brain. This objective can be realized by injecting into the brain a dye that is very opaque in that it can absorb a lot of the X rays. However, the injection is not directly into the brain through the skull bone. Rather, the dye is introduced into the artery that pumps blood into the brain. You can locate this artery (the carotid artery) if you place your hands on your neck, near each side of the windpipe, and feel a pulse beating. Once the radiopaque dye enters the blood circulation, it is fed into the brain very quickly. The kind of picture that can then be obtained is called an angiogram. Angiograms give a clear readout of the pattern of branching blood vessels that go through all the brain regions.

Now imagine there is damage to the cerebral circulation—for example, if someone has a stroke where there is a blockage or a narrowing of the blood vessel walls. This problem will then show up on the angiogram. Similarly, if a patient has a tumor it will sometimes push blood vessels away and the abnormal positioning due to the displacement will be detectable to a trained eye. In this way, angiograms are very valuable diagnostic tools that offer a way of circumventing the problem of the insensitivity of X rays to brain tissue. But what if the blood vessels are functioning normally? It could be that there are problems with the brain, but the blood circulation is not where the problem lies. Then angiograms will not be helpful.

The alternative to making the brain more radiopaque is to make the method of detection more sensitive. With normal X rays there are about twenty to thirty variations on the gray scale; but a technique was developed in the early 1970s with more than two hundred variations and has been routinely used since the early 1980s: computerized axial tomography (CAT).

In CAT, brain X rays are taken in a series of sections or scans. The patient lies with his or her head in a cylinder with an X-ray tube on one side and an X-ray beam on the other, and these two devices are placed around the head. The X ray does not strike a photographic plate but rather a sensor that is connected to a computer; this sensor is far more sensitive than the photographic plate used in ordinary X rays. All the measurements are taken and assembled by computer to give a scan. The tube moves along the axis of the body and this procedure is repeated eight or nine times.

The kind of pictures that can be seen by CAT scans give neurologists and brain surgeons a valuable indication of the location and extent of tumors and tissue loss. For example, CAT scans have recently given a clue toward understanding the degenerative disorder of Alzheimer's disease, where there is severe confusion and loss of memory. A. D. Smith and K. A. Jobst found that in Alzheimer patients a certain brain region (the medial temporal lobe) gradually decreased over time to about half the width of that in healthy volunteers of the same age ("Use of structural imaging to study the progression of Alzheimer's disease," *British Medical Bulletin* 52, 575–86). Not only does such an observation indicate the brain region that should be targeted for developing possible therapies for this debilitating disorder, but it has enormous diagnostic potential for revealing the start of brain damage before the clinical symptoms of memory loss have become clearly apparent.

Despite the fact that X rays have been familiar to us for most of the twentieth century, their use in CAT scans and angiograms has been invaluable for investigating brain damage. However, there are limits to the type of brain dysfunction that can be studied in this way. X rays detect abnormalities in the anatomical properties of the brain. If you have a CAT scan it will tell you whether you have something physically wrong *and enduring* within your brain, such as a tumor or a lesion. But if the problem is functional rather than anatomical—something to do with the actual operations of the brain—X rays will not tell you what bits of your brain are working at particular times during a particular task. How might this problem be overcome?

Of all the organs of the body, the brain is the greediest in its fuel consumption. It burns oxygen and glucose at ten times the rate of all other body tissues at rest. In fact, the brain uses up so much energy that it dies if deprived of oxygen for only a few minutes. Even though the brain is less than 2.5 percent of our total body weight, it is responsible for 20 percent of energy consumption at rest. But what happens to this energy? It enables the brain to "work."

When a brain region is working, it uses up much more fuel. The fuel for the brain is the carbohydrates in the food that you eat and the oxygen in the air that you breathe: when carbohydrates react with oxygen, they generate carbon dioxide, water, and most important of all, heat. In the body, all the energy from food is not released immediately in a simple combustion, because it would not be very helpful if there was no energy left for any of the functions of the brain and body. Thus, although some heat is needed to keep us warm, there is a chemical in the body that prevents the immediate release of all the energy from food we have eaten. Through its formation we are able to store up this energy for the mechanical, electrical, and chemical work that the body and the brain has to do. The energy-storing chemical adenosine triphosphate (ATP) is produced from the food we eat for as long as we are alive. ATP stores energy and has the potential to liberate it like a compressed spring upon release.

If brain regions are active during a particular task, they are working hard and using more energy; they are making great demand on ATP stores, and hence more carbohydrates, the simplest form of which is glucose, as well as oxygen are required. It follows that if we could trace the increased demand for oxygen or for glucose by certain parts of the brain, we would be able to say what brain areas were most active or working hardest during any particular task. This is the principle of the two particular techniques used to visualize the brain actually at work.

One technique is known as positron emission tomography (PET). The basic requirement in PET is for either oxygen or glucose to be labeled so that it can be easily tracked. The "label" in this case is a radioactive atom, in the sense that it contains an unstable nucleus that ejects positrons at very high speed. Positrons are fundamental particles similar to electrons except that they have a positive charge. Radioactive oxygen atoms incorporated into either glucose or water molecules are injected intravenously. The radioactive label is then carried by the blood into the brain. The emitted positrons collide with electrons in other molecules within the brain and mutually annihilate each other. The burst of energy that results forms a gamma ray that is of sufficiently high energy to penetrate through the skull and be detected outside of the head.

Because these high-energy gamma rays can travel a long way, they pass right out of the head and strike sensors, the signal from which is then used to build up an image of the brain at work. The glucose or oxygen accumulates in the brain regions that need it most, namely those working the hardest. With PET, it is possible to show different active areas according to tasks as subtly different as saying words compared with reading words. (See Figure 3.)

A second imaging technique, functional magnetic resonance imaging (MRI), is like PET in that it relies on the differential expenditure of energy by whatever brain regions are working hardest; however, this time no injections are involved. Because there is no problem with ascertaining exactly when the injected label reaches the brain, imaging

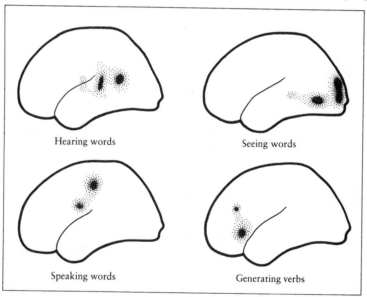

FIGURE 3

The interactive brain. A drawing representing a positron emission tomography (PET) scan of a conscious human subject performing similar but subtly different tasks. Note that although the tasks are all linked to language, different brain regions will be involved according to the precise nature of the undertaking. Note also that at no time is just one brain region active completely on its own.

[Adapted from Greenfield, *Journey to the Centers of the Mind*]

with MRI has the potential to give an even more faithful re-
flection of what is going on at a given moment. MRI, like
PET, also measures changes in blood oxygen concentration
serving brain areas that are more active; however, the
method of detection is different. Oxygen is carried by the
protein hemoglobin. MRI exploits the fact that the actual
amount of oxygen present affects the magnetic properties
of hemoglobin: these properties can be monitored in the
presence of a magnetic field, where the nuclei of the atoms
line up as though they were themselves miniature magnets.
When bombarded and pushed out of alignment by radio
waves, these atoms emit radio signals as they spin back
into line. The radio signal is unique to the amount of oxygen carried by hemoglobin in the sample and therefore
gives a very sensitive measure of the activity of different regions of the brain. This technique can pinpoint an area as
small as 1 to 2 millimeters and measure events taking place
over seconds.

With the use of these techniques it is becoming increasingly apparent that during a specific task several different
brain regions are working simultaneously. There is not just
one brain area for one function but rather several brain areas appear to contribute to a particular function. Moreover,
if some aspect of the task changes slightly, such as hearing
words rather than speaking words, then a different constel-
lation of brain regions appears.

Brain events are monitored over a time scale exceeding
several seconds and averaged over, at best, a cubic millimeter of tissue. Another method, magnetoencephalography
(MEG), measures the magnetic field generated by differential electrical activity of the brain and has a superior time
resolution, but is only currently accurate for the outer regions of the brain. Although their true potential lies in the
future, when the space and time resolutions are more com-
mensurate with the scale of real brain cells, techniques
such as PET, MRI, and MEG are already offering windows

to the brain at work. Perhaps the most obvious lesson they have taught us so far is that it is misleading to think of one brain region as having one specific, autonomous function, as in the phrenologists' scenario. Instead, different brain regions combine in some way to work in parallel for different functions.

The brain is made up of anatomically distinct regions, but these regions are not autonomous minibrains; rather, they constitute a cohesive and integrated system organized for the most part in a mysterious way. Therefore, it will be almost impossible to learn how the brain works by studying just one particular region at a time. Instead, let us start with specific and familiar functions and trace how their processing is parceled out between multiple areas in the brain.

....

CHAPTER 2

SYSTEMS OF SYSTEMS

Every waking moment we are bombarded with sights, sounds, and smells as we touch, run, climb, and speak our way through life. Animal existence is one of constant dialogue with the outside world. The brain is vital for processing and coordinating the information that floods in through the senses, with the outputs of the brain expressed as movements. But how is it all achieved? In the previous chapter we saw that there was no single center in the brain directly corresponding to each and every function or behavior in the outside world. In this chapter we shall explore the riddle of how function is localized in the brain by starting not with brain regions but with the functions themselves.

Charles Sherrington, one of the greatest pioneers of physiology during the first half of this century, summed up the all-pervasive contribution of movement to our lives: "From a whisper in the forest to a felling of a tree, 'tis all movement." From the subtleties of body language to the precision of the spoken word to the unambiguity of a simple hug, virtually all communication relies on movement. However global or imperceptible, all movement depends on the contraction of some muscle group somewhere in the body. If contraction of all muscle is defunct, all that is left is the ability to drool or shed tears.

Although plants can move in the sense that they may turn to the light, they cannot generate movements as we do. Outside the realm of science fiction, no plant locomotes from one place to another. In clear contrast, all animals are on the move—that is, they are *animated*. Interestingly enough, the Latin *animus* means "consciousness."

If you move about and you are a multicellular organism, then you have, at the very least, a primitive kind of brain. The importance for moving creatures of having some kind of brain is best illustrated by an observation initially made by the late Emperor Hirohito of Japan, for whom the study of marine life was a passionate hobby. The tunicate in question is known as a sea squirt. When it is an immature larva the sea squirt spends its time swimming around: not only is it capable of coordinated movement but it also has a primitive vibration-sensitive device, crudely comparable with an ear, and a primitive light-sensitive device, roughly analogous to an eye. In fact, the sea squirt could be said to have a modest brain. However, when it becomes mature the sea squirt changes its lifestyle and attaches to a rock. It no longer has to swim around anymore, because it now lives by filtering seawater. At this stage the sea squirt actually performs the remarkable act of consuming its own brain.

The clue to brain function provided by this tale is that you only need a brain when you are moving. For stationary life forms, a brain is no longer necessary. The whole point is that for an animal moving around, there is an interaction with an environment that is incessantly changing. You need a device to tell you very quickly what is happening and, most importantly, to enable you to respond to what is happening, to get out of the way of predators or to chase after prey. So the brain, in whatever shape, size, and degree of sophistication, is somehow connected in a very basic way to ensuring survival as both a consequence and a cause of movement. According to the lifestyle of the animal, there are different types of movement. The trapeze artistry of the swinging monkey, the precision gliding of the eagle, and the coordination of the legs on a millipede are examples of specialized movement accommodating particular lifestyles.

How is movement of any sort actually achieved? The contraction of the appropriate muscle occurs following a signal sent down from the brain, along the spinal cord. Nerves controlling all the different muscles leave the spinal cord in an ordered fashion, according to the location of the muscle in the body. People with injuries to their spine are unable to move to varying extents according to the level at which the spinal cord is damaged.

Sometimes the spinal cord can function more or less autonomously, without descending instructions or control from the brain. Such movements are reflexes. A reflex can be defined as a fixed response to a particular trigger—the most obvious example is the knee jerk. The knee jerk reflex is triggered when the knee is tapped and in response the lower leg shoots out. Neuroscientists refer to this familiar sequence of events as the "stretch reflex" because the tap at the critical point on the knee in effect compresses a tendon by which the muscle in the lower leg is suspended, thereby exerting extra pressure on the muscle and stretching it. In order to compensate for this lengthening, the muscle contracts, so that the leg shoots forward.

Our normal repertoire of movement is not one of fixed responses to rather artificial triggers like the neurologist's delicate hammer. We do not wait for someone to tap our knee so that we might jerk our leg. Many of the movements that we make—such as walking, swimming, and running—involve a more complex coordination of muscle groups. But even these movements are, in a sense, semiautomatic. These kind of rhythmic, subconscious movements are caused by signals coming down from the brain stem (see Chapter 1). Different groups of neurons in this brain stem region send signals down the spinal cord to cause the appropriate contraction of muscles in a repeating sequence.

There are four such brain motorways coming down the spinal cord from the brain stem. One is responsible for semireflex rhythmic movements, like swimming, while another coordinates movement with visual and sensory information; yet another is important for balance, while the fourth motorway mediates the moving of individual limbs. There is, however, yet a further type of movement that we tend to take for granted and that is not controlled by any of these four systems: fine movement of the fingers. Dexterity with our hand distinguishes primates from all other animals. It enables us to fashion and use tools and thus to attain a lifestyle that other species will never be able to realize. The dexterity of a violinist, for example, where fast, controlled, independent movement of the digits is critical, is a spectacular feat of evolution.

Unlike the other descending spinal routes used for the contraction of muscle, the messages instigating and controlling fine finger movement do not originate from the brain stem at the top of the spinal cord but from the very top of the brain, a striplike region of the cortex fitting across the brain a little like a hairband, and known as the motor cortex (see Chapter 1). The motor cortex controls fine movements by sending signals directly to the digits in question. It also indirectly influences movements by sending other signals to the four motorway centers in the brain stem, which in turn activate the appropriate contraction of muscle. Different parts of the motor cortex are allocated to controlling different parts of the body. It might be assumed that such an allocation would correspond to the size of the body part in question—that is, a tiny area such as the hand would be controlled by only a tiny part of motor cortex, whereas a large area like the back would have the lion's share of motor cortex to control its movements. However, nothing could be further from the truth.

The critical factor turns out to be the precision of the movement that the body part needs to make. The more precise the movements generated, the larger the area of the brain that is devoted to them. Hence the hands and the mouth have an enormous allocation within the motor cortex compared with the upper arm and the small of the back, which do not seem to have much representation at all. The kind of movements you make with your back are not that fine or precise. (See Figure 4.)

The motor cortex is pivotal to the generation of movement: not only does it have direct control of some of the muscles controlling the hands, and hence of precision movements, but it also exerts a hierarchical influence over the other four movement motorways. In the previous chapter the idea of a single command center for any one function was rejected, but surely here it seems that the motor cortex is well qualified to be the "Movement Center" of the brain.

Not quite. Although the motor cortex plays a critical role in the control of movement, it does not have a monopoly. Two other areas would also be worthy contenders for the title of movement center: the basal ganglia and the cerebellum. If either of these regions, which are far away from the motor cortex, is damaged, then movement is dramatically impaired in various ways.

The cerebellum, the little brain at the back of the main brain, was seen in Chapter 1 to have a function that presumably dominates the lifestyle of cockerels and fish far more than it does our own. Pecking at food or swimming through the sea necessitates an ability to coordinate the information constantly coming in through the senses with appropriate movements. There is no time for thinking or planning a movement as other animals loom close to the crumbs in the barnyard. Perhaps then the cerebellum is important for automated movements triggered by outside events rather than by internalized proactive thought processes.

It is quite remarkable that as long ago as 1664 the physician Thomas Willis had also formed this view of the cerebellum, which he referred to as the cerebel. Willis viewed the cerebellum as a truly isolated structure from the rest of the brain, responsible for unconscious movements:

> The Cerebel is a peculiar fountain of animal Spirits designed for some works, wholly distinct from the Brain. Within the Brain . . . all the spontaneous motions, to wit, of which we are knowing and willing, are per-

FIGURE 4

Reconstructions of the human body in accordance with the space in the cortex devoted to each body part for moving. Note how the mouth and the hands have the greatest number of brain cells controlling them.

[Courtesy of the British Museum of Natural History]

formed. . . . But the spirits inhabiting the Cerebel perform unperceivedly and silently their works of Nature
without our knowledge or care [Willis, T., Cerebi
anatome: cui accessit nervorum descriptio et usus (London: J. Martyn and J. Allistry, 1664), p.111].

Three hundred years later, this description could still
apply. Patients with damage to the cerebellum can move,
but in a clumsy way. They have particular difficulty with
movements requiring the type of sensory motor coordination that characterizes skilled movements such as playing
the piano or dancing. The cerebellum is important for
movements where there is a continuous feedback from
your senses, which in turn will trigger or influence the
next type of movement. Imagine, for example, that you
have to trace a complex pattern onto paper. Your hand is
under constant surveillance from your eyes. People with
cerebellar damage find this tracking movement particularly hard.

Humans engage in many more sophisticated activities
not dependent on the immediate triggers in the environment. Our more flexible and versatile repertoire of movement reduces the centrality of the cerebellum in terms of
the fraction of our brain it constitutes compared to the
cockerel or the fish. The cerebellum is nonetheless of vital
importance since the sensory motor coordination it generates underpins skilled movements that are also the type of
movements not requiring conscious thought. These movements improve with practice to become almost subconscious. For this reason the cerebellum has been dubbed the
"autopilot" of the brain. This epithet fits closely with the
description long ago formulated by Willis.

There is another type of subconscious movement that is
not modified by updated information from the senses. Unlike movements controlled by the cerebellum, those associated with the basal ganglia cannot be changed once they

have been initiated. These "ballistic" movements resemble a cannonball exploding out of a cannon mouth: once started, it cannot be stopped and its trajectory cannot be modified. When someone takes a golf swing, the ball might stay mockingly on the tee because the movement cannot be corrected at the last moment: it is, literally, hit or miss.

The area of the brain associated with these ballistic movements, the basal ganglia, is really a group of various interconnected brain regions. When any of these regions are damaged, there are devastating consequences for movement. According to the part of the basal ganglia that is impaired, there can be wild, involuntary movements (Huntington's chorea), or the exact opposite, difficulty in moving at all, combined with muscle rigidity and tremor (Parkinson's disease). Huntington's chorea and Parkinson's disease affect two different parts of the basal ganglia (the striatum and substantia nigra respectively) that seem to normally work in a kind of power-balancing act, locked together so that the first region counteracts the second, a little like a seesaw or arm wrestling. Normally, as with a seesaw or with arm wrestling between two equally matched individuals, one brain region keeps the other in check.

But imagine a scenario in which one person on a seesaw is much lighter, or an arm-wrestling opponent is much weaker, than his or her colleague: the balance collapses. Hence if one brain region is underactive, the other becomes too active. It is this imbalance in activity that appears to lead to abnormal movements. In the case of Huntington's chorea, the deficient region in the dialogue is toward the front of the brain, the striatum; on the other hand, in Parkinson's disease, it is the moustache-shaped, black-pigmented region toward the back of the brain, the substantia nigra, that is less dominant.

Because these two regions are normally so closely linked with each other, any drug that restores the balance of power between them will be effective. In Parkinson's disease, drugs that dampen activity in the striatum have a similar effect to those enhancing activity in the substantia nigra. Conversely, any drug that reduces activity in the substantia nigra or enhances activity in the striatum is pernicious in Parkinson's disease but highly beneficial in Huntington's chorea. Even within one general brain region, the basal ganglia, the component parts themselves are not autonomous but are functioning in an incessant dialogue with each other.

Thus, there is no single movement center after all. Rather, movement can be split up—although we are not consciously aware of it happening—into different types that are in turn controlled by different basic brain areas. However, even these different brain areas, such as the cerebellum and basal ganglia, do not function as autonomous units, but are in turn in dialogue with different parts of the outer layer of the brain, the cortex. The cerebellum, for example, has strong connections with a part of the cortex that lies distinct from, and in front of, the motor cortex (lateral premotor area), while the basal ganglia are in intimate contact with yet another area of cortex known as the supplementary motor area. Indeed, damage to the supplementary motor area can lead to impairments strikingly similar to Parkinson's disease.

In the normal situation, an attractive though speculative scenario is to view the subcortical regions as controlling the movements that do not rely on any contribution of conscious thought. For example, pressing the brake when the traffic lights are red seems to be an automatic movement, which is in fact associated with the cerebellum. In contrast, if you finally decide to drag yourself out of the armchair on a Sunday afternoon, the actual movement requires very little conscious planning. There is no immediate sensory trigger, but the standing up is automatic nonetheless. Some neuroscientists even go so far as to refer to this type of movement as a "motor program." Whatever the label, this type of internally triggered movement that most of us take for granted is controlled by the basal ganglia. It is particularly hard, however, for a Parkinsonian patient. The basal ganglia and cerebellum in these cases are freeing up the cortex for other roles beyond the minute-by-minute task of motor control. On the other hand, some movements, be they ballistic or sensory triggered, might require different degrees of conscious control. In this case the supplementary motor area and lateral premotor area dominate more fully in the respective dialogues over their subcortical partners, the basal ganglia or cerebellum.

The generation of movement is the net result of many brain regions acting together as individual instruments do in a symphony. The type of movement being made, and whether it requires conscious control, determines exactly which brain regions are involved, while pathologies such as Parkinson's disease have highlighted the consequences of dialogues between brain regions becoming too one-sided.

But the idea of a "center" for different functions in the brain is so intuitively appealing, it is hard to relinquish. We might have more luck with the senses. Unlike with movement, the senses offer us a clear stimulus—be it a light, a bang, a pinch, or the taste of raspberries—where we can trace the fate of a "signal" as it is processed at different stages in the brain. Perhaps such a clear path will lead us, naturally, to a final vision center, hearing center, and so on.

Just as there are motorways leaving the brain via the spinal cord to control muscles and hence movement, so there are incoming signals that, as we saw in Chapter 1, are sent up the spinal cord into the brain. These signals relate to touch and pain, and are referred to as the somatosensory system. Triggered by the point of contact where, for example, a pin pierces the skin, local nerves within the skin transmit signals to the spinal cord. These signals are then relayed up from the spinal cord and finally arrive at the outermost reaches of the brain, in an area of cortex just behind the motor cortex known as the somatosensory cortex.

There are two major motorways heading up the spinal cord for the somatosensory cortex: one, the evolutionary system, is chiefly related to pain and temperature, while the newer system carries precise signals relating to touch. This arrangement has an intuitive appeal in that it makes sense for the more basic, established system to be concerned with basic survival factors such as pain and temperature, whereas the more refined skills involving precision of touch would become increasingly important as the organism evolved.

Different neurons in the somatosensory cortex correspond to touch in different parts of the body. You might expect that your hand, which is a relatively small part of your body, would have neurons that register impulses in a very small part of the cortex. However, just as we saw for the motor cortex, there is no direct matching of an area of your body to an area of the somatosensory cortex. The hands and the mouth have an enormous, vastly disproportionate representation.

This biased allocation of neurons makes sense. Just as the hands and mouth claim a large allocation of neurons in the motor cortex to enable violin playing and speaking, so those same parts of the body lionize large proportions of neurons in the somatosensory cortex. It is important for the mouth and hands to be most sensitive to touch because eating and feeling things with the hands are among the most basic human behaviors. If you have had a local anesthetic at the dentist, you know how debilitated you feel at not being sensitive to movement or touch in even a small area of the mouth.

This difference in sensitivity to touch on different parts of the body can be demonstrated very easily. If a pair of compass points are set relatively near each other and placed lightly on different parts of the body, they will be perceived either as one point or two according to where they are placed, even though the distance between them remains constant. In the small of the back, for example, where the sensitivity is modest due to the modest allocation of cells in the cortex, two points relatively close are felt as just one. By contrast, when the points are placed on the tips of the fingers, there is a sufficient number of corresponding neurons in the cortex to relay an adequately sensitive message that there are two points. The allocation of the brain to coordinating parts of the body depends on the importance of that part of the body to the task at hand. But how does the brain deal with inputs through specialized organs that do not rely on messages being passed up the spinal cord or on different contributions from different parts of the body? How do we even begin to see and hear?

In simpler nervous systems with much simpler lifestyles there is no need for a rich tapestry of visual scenes. A frog would benefit little from being able to distinguish the fine detail of the Mona Lisa, for example. In the frog world, all a frog wants to know is if there are predators or prey: its retina has accordingly become sensitive only to shadows, which would be cast by predators or prey that it can eat, namely flies moving backward and forward. Fine detail of objects is irrelevant and therefore simply not registered by the frog's eyes. When presented with a piece of cork dangling on a string, crudely resembling a fly flitting past, a frog will make all the predatory and gustatory movements not only of sticking out its tongue to catch the fly but of licking it lips as well.

As a general rule in the animal kingdom, the more complex or relatively big the eye in relation to the body, then the smaller the rest of the brain. More processing will go on at the earliest stages, in the peripheral organ, than in more sophisticated brains where the input will not have already been heavily biased. Insects have compound eyes that look a little like geodesic domes arranged on each side of the head. Each eye consists of some ten thousand distinct modules amounting to ten thousand facets all angled in different directions. Some insects have up to thirty thousand such facets. Light is funneled through each module, so that there is a huge magnification. However, in human terms the results would be far from ideal as the lenses of these facets cannot be focused. The huge advantage for the insect is that a large visual field is projected onto a small number of cells without the insect moving its head. The more facets, the more detailed the picture. This type of eye is very sensitive to any change in the visual scene and to the planes of light polarization; however, the compound eye cannot give a high degree of resolution.

The human eye is very different: it is ball shaped and consists of two main sections, separated by the lens. The lens is a transparent, elastic convex structure that is suspended by ligaments to control its shape, and this shape can change from one moment to the next according to whether you want to look a long way off or a short distance. With the cornea at the very front of the eye, the lens helps us to focus. The colored iris, which varies greatly between individuals, regulates light by constricting or dilating the pupil. The gap between the cornea and the lens in this front part of the eye is filled with a watery fluid. By contrast, in the second compartment comprising the main body of the eye, the cavity is filled with a jellylike substance.

At the very back of the eye is the retina, which is the image-detecting zone. If you look at the retina under a microscope, there is a tangle of cells seemingly forming a jumbled mass that looks a little like a net—hence the name *retina,* from the Latin *retus* for "net." These cells in the retina respond to changes of light by a change in an electrical signal passed on to two more relays of cells before being transmitted into the brain proper, via the bundle of fibers known as the optic nerve.

The exit point where this nerve leaves the retina and burrows into the brain is the "blind spot" where there is obviously no room for light-sensitive cells. The blind spot is just to the side of the middle of the eye, near the nose. On the other side of the middle of the eye, near the ear, is an area of the retina called the fovea. The fovea is a small indent where there is a high concentration of a certain type of cells that are sensitive to light. If light strikes this area, vision is optimal as there are more cells here to do the job. Birds of prey can have up to five times more concentrated cells in their fovea than humans. In addition, unlike humans, eagles have two foveas. One, the search fovea, is for sideway vision, whereas the pursuit fovea judges depth, which is done with both eyes.

Unlike human eyes, all bird eyes are fixed in their sockets. In order to turn their eyes, birds have to turn their entire head and neck. Our lifestyle would be drastically compromised if we were unable to move our eyes back and forth without moving our head—imagine reading, for example! For both the eagle and humans, however, light (electromagnetic waves) travels through the eyeball and penetrates the outer two layers of the retina to be processed by the light-sensitive cells. The particular cells sensitive to color are known as cones, and the other type of light-sensitive cells are referred to as rods. These rods are for vision in darkened conditions, leaving three types of cone to respond principally to one of three primary colors: red, green, or blue. Within the electromagnetic spectrum, our human eyes detect only a very small section as visible light: between 400 and 700 nanometers on a scale varying between 10 meters, the wavelength of an AM radio, and less than a nanometer, the wavelength range in which we find X rays and gamma rays.

How is light actually registered in the brain? It must first be converted by the retina into electrical impulses. In the dark there is a steady release of a chemical messenger from the rods onto the next relay of cells within the retina. When light first strikes, it is absorbed by a special chemical (rhodopsin) within the rod. The ensuing change in this chemical caused by the absorption of light then triggers a cascade of chemical reactions inside the cell. The end result of these reactions within the rod is a change in its electrical properties.

It is this change in electrical properties, namely the voltage normally generated by the rod, that changes the message it had been transmitting as long as there was darkness. In the case of the other type of light-sensitive cells, the cones, we start to process color by the selectivity of different cones responding to certain ranges of light with peak sensitivities for red, green, or blue wavelengths. Different colors excite different combinations of these cones in different proportions. For example, a certain wavelength excites red and green cones in equal numbers and is perceived as yellow.

We have seen that electromagnetic waves are converted by cells in the retina into electrical signals. However, the retina does not just signal uniformly and equally everything in your visual field. The image is relayed into the brain with an enormous bias. For example, if there is a large uniform area within an object, then only weak signals are passed on, whereas if there is contrast the visual signals are most vigorous. The retina is really only concerned with detecting change. But change does not just occur in space, with contrasting edges; there is also change in time, namely movement. The retina can adapt so that it no longer responds to stationary objects while still retaining the ability to signal for movement. To appreciate the preference of the nervous system for states of change, think of how a flashing light is more noticeable than a constant one. Our survival may well depend on a change in the surrounding situation much more than if everything remains the same.

The eyeball itself is not a self-contained center for vision; rather, it is the gateway by which the all-important signals gain access to the brain for further processing before we can actually see. From the retina, cells send out electrical signals along the fibers, exiting via the blind spot, deep into the brain, to the *thalamus,* meaning "room" in Greek. This brain structure, which occupies a substantial part of the middle section of the brain (the diencephalon), then relays the signals to the visual cortex, the outer layer at the back of the head. Studies of people who have lost parts of the visual cortex have given neuroscientists some very helpful and intriguing insights into understanding what might happen in this area that enables us to see.

For example, a stroke victim in her forties had cells damaged in a highly localized region within the visual cortex. Although she could see all stationary objects as well as anyone else, she was unable to see objects in motion. If, for example, she poured tea, it apparently seemed frozen like a glacier. Indeed she was unable to engage in this activity because she could not stop pouring: she could not see the level of the fluid in the cup rising sufficiently well to know when to stop. This patient also said that when she spoke to people, conversation proved a problem because she was unaware of the movements of the mouth of the speaker. Even worse, and more dangerous, she was unable to monitor the progress of a car: first it was in one place and then suddenly it was almost on top of her. On the other hand, this woman could detect movement through her sense of sound or touch.

Comparable situations have been reported since World War I, when people came under the scrutiny of doctors following head injuries due to the wounds of battle. A physician of the time, George Riddoch, studied these patients: he reported that there were people who could see movement, unlike the lady we have just been discussing, but not shape or color. Often anyone with normal vision can experience this phenomenon: if something moves in your extreme peripheral vision, you are aware of movement, but you then need to turn your head to see exactly what it was that moved.

Similarly, there are those who can see form and movement but cannot experience color. A world composed entirely of shades of gray would be the fate of people who had either a deficit of cones in the retina or damage to critical regions on both sides of their head. If the brain is only damaged on one side, however, then half the world appears in color and half the world is in black and white.

Finally, some patients with damage to the visual system can see movement and color but not form. *Agnosia,* from the Greek meaning "failure to recognize," is a condition characterized by the ability to see objects without identifying them. Agnosia can vary in its severity from patient to patient, and even the same patient may have better form vision from time to time. The vision expert Semir Zeki suggests one reason this particular condition can be so variable: if complex forms were to be gradually assembled in our brains from less complex patterns, then perhaps this gradual process of construction could be arrested at different stages in different people. Some patients would thus have a more extensive visual repertoire than others. Zeki suggests that understanding and seeing are not two separate processes but rather they are inextricably linked: if you see something you will automatically identify it. On the other hand, if you do not see an object in front of you, Zeki argues that it is because there has been a collapse of the higher integrative processes for complex form recognition in the visual cortex. Obviously, you will not recognize the object. You will be to a greater or lesser extent "form blind."

After considering the cases just presented, it is evident that vision of form, movement, and color can occur independently of each other. Current thinking is that we

process vision at least partly in parallel, that is, we are processing visual signals simultaneously but in different parts
of the brain. Different aspects of our vision, form, color,
and movement seem to us a cohesive whole, but are actually processed, at least in part, by different systems connecting through relays from the retina to the back of the
head. Thus, as we saw in the case of movement, we can see
that different regions of the brain are working together to
contribute to what we regard as a single function, in this
case seeing. The big mystery is how does it all come together again? Where in the brain do we make all the parallel visual signals converge into a single entity?

Some people have suggested that there is a convergence
of these different pathways in certain parts of the brain,
like railway tracks leading into Grand Central Station. This
scenario is, in a sense, a late–twentieth century version of
the doctrine of phrenology discussed in the previous chapter. Just imagine that we possessed the brain equivalent of
one or two Grand Central Stations in our heads: if such an
area were damaged, then it follows that vision would be
completely lost. But this scenario never occurs. Thus, we
have yet a further example of how the brain is not organized as a simple bundle of minibrains. The connections
between brain regions are not directed to converge into an
executive center but are more likely to take the form of balanced dialogues between key brain regions, comparable to
what we saw for the control of movement.

Yet in itself this scenario of interactive, parallel brain
regions does not solve one of the greatest mysteries of neuroscience: How do we actually see? On the one hand, great
strides have been made in understanding the complex
steps in the visual processing of an object: it is now known
what parts of the brain, during vision, are active at what
times and under what conditions. But such responses can
persist even when the brain is anesthetized, when there is
no consciousness at all. No one has yet pointed to a single

event that occurs in awake but not anesthetized brains where the intervention of consciousness into the visual process could be identified as an unambiguous physiological/anatomical mechanism or event.

The riddle is compounded by observations where there is a conspicuous dissociation of brain visual processes and conscious awareness in fully awake patients. The first condition was again reported initially as a result of head wounds in World War I and was later dubbed blind sight in the 1970s. Blind-sight patients are blind in a certain part of their visual field, but if asked to "guess," they can nevertheless point to objects, which they claim they cannot see, placed in that area. Clearly the brain is still functioning, but the consciousness is lost of actually seeing the object. Some, such as Zeki and the physicist Eric Harth, have argued that the anatomical integrity of neuronal circuits is all-important. As we saw earlier, brain regions can be viewed as participants on a seesaw, where the balance between them, their interaction, is more critical than any individual region on its own. Harth suggests that not only are signals relating to the senses conveyed for processing to the cortex but in turn the cortex can send signals that intercept this incoming stream of information, to modify it. The more vigorous the cortical interception, the more idiosyncratic and remote from objective external events will be the final conscious experience. Zeki also makes uses of these feedback pathways in his interpretation of blind sight.

Zeki suggests that blind sight is due to a rupture in this balanced circuitry. The processing of the signals can still be relayed into the brain, but conscious vision is abolished since certain pathways normally sustaining dialogue upon dialogue between brain regions are no longer operational. However, this idea does not square entirely with a particularly interesting observation concerning blind-sight patients: the actual degree of physical damage to certain brain regions need not be the only factor in determining how a blind-sight patient will respond. In certain cases blind sight can be reversed by other factors: for example, if an otherwise stationary object is made to move. Perhaps then, for a final consciousness of seeing an object, not only are intact neuronal circuits important but also the particular properties of the object in question.

Another example of brain damage that leads to vision deficit is a condition that is the reverse of blindsight: *prosopagnosia,* from the Greek meaning "failure to recognize faces." Whereas blind sight entails recognition without awareness, this condition is one of awareness without recognition. Patients can see faces as faces, but cannot recognize anyone, even themselves. There can be a marked difference if a face is made psychologically "stronger" by presenting faces that are linked. For example, if a picture of Princess Diana is presented after that of her ex-husband, Prince Charles, a patient can often recognize Diana's face. Again we have an example of consciousness being dependent on more than one factor, but we still have no idea how such factors lead to the seemingly magic step within the brain that enables us not only to process an object registered by our retina but to consciously see it as well.

For all the senses there is also the enigma of the nature of the first-person subjective conscious element. There is much more to hearing, for example, than mere vibrations. We do not hear a symphony as vibrations any more than we see a face as lines and contrast. Rather, our perceptions are unified wholes, shot through with memories, hopes, prejudices, and other internalized cognitive idiosyncrasies.

Another tantalizing and related mystery of the brain is why electrical signals arriving in the visual cortex should be experienced as vision, while exactly the same kind of electrical signals, arriving in another part of the brain such as the somatosensory cortex or the auditory cortex, should be perceived as touch and hearing respectively. No one has yet given a satisfactory explanation, although one idea is that we learn through experience to distinguish sound from sight; another idea is that each sensory system is linked preferentially in some way to certain types of movement, which emphasizes the distinction.

However, there are well-known examples of where this distinction between the senses falls down, a mixing of the senses known as synesthesia. People displaying synesthesia may claim to "see" certain musical notes in certain colors. Virtually any combination of two of the five senses is possible, although it is the experience of different colors upon hearing different sounds that is the most common. Synesthesia tends to occur more in childhood, but can often be triggered in adults with psychotic disorders such as schizophrenia or by hallucinatory drugs. The division of the senses then is clearly attributable to some aspect of normal brain organization, but an aspect that is not immune to individual perturbation. One possibility is that there are additional connections in the brain of the synesthetic that extend not only from the sense organ in question to the cortex appropriate for that modality but also innervate another cortical sense area as well. This idea, however, is not very likely as it would not account for the variability in synesthetic experiences, namely that such states only occur under certain conditions. It is more likely that the areas of the cortex not allocated to the primary processing of each of the individual senses, namely the association cortex, somehow play a part.

We saw in Chapter 1 that even compared to the brain of our nearest relative, the chimpanzee, the areas of human brain classified as association cortex are vast. It is possible that inputs from association cortex into the areas of cortex devoted to particular senses might in some way be aberrant. Certainly such a scenario would account for the greater predominance of synesthesia in children, before distinctions between the senses are learned and where the neurons of the brain are less hard wired and thus more flexible and versatile in their operations, as we shall see in Chapter 4. A malfunctioning of physiology (the working of neurons) rather than anatomy (their physical connections) would also explain why synesthesia can suddenly appear in the brain of a schizophrenic. On the other hand, any real explanation of synesthesia is impossible as it hinges on a subjective perspective: the firsthand experience of an individual. Synesthesia is a facet of consciousness, that ultimate riddle of the brain.

So far we have seen how that private inner world of one's own consciousness is influenced by sensory input pouring in and reflected in an output movement. By being able to receive detailed and incessant information about our environment, and responding quickly and appropriately to each individual situation, we are in a constant dialogue with the outside world. A further factor in determining how vigorous and effective this dialogue may be is level of arousal. When asleep, we perceive nothing of the world around us, nor are we moving about; at the other end of the spectrum, high arousal leads to distracted behavior where we overreact to a minor occurrence and move about in a restless, purposeless way. Psychologists have long found that we are most efficient at performing tasks when we are in the middle range level of arousal. Arousal then is an important consideration to our prevailing state of mind.

We are familiar with the extremes of arousal: when we sleep, arousal levels are low; if we are overactive and easily distracted, with a racing heart and sweaty palms, we are overexcited or overaroused. Arousal is with us all the time, to varying degrees. It is governed by distinct groups of different chemicals in the brain stem that predominate at different times of the day and night, or with emotions or illness, and that send signals up to the large regions of cortex to modulate, on a global scale, the workings of many circuits of brain cells. One measure of arousal can be monitored as changes in the ensuing electrical activity averaged over large areas of the cortex.

As long ago as 1875, weak electrical currents were recorded from the brains of rabbits and monkeys by an English physiologist, Richard Caton. The finding triggered little attention. Fifteen years later, however, controversy flared between a Polish physiologist, A. Beck, and an Austrian, E. Fleischel Von Marxow, who each laid claims to discovering electrical activity in the brain. It was only when Caton settled the matter by pointing to his much older publication in the *British Medical Journal* that the finding was duly recognized. The clinical implications of this discovery were not to be realized until fifty years later, when in 1929 a German psychiatrist, Hans Berger, first attempted to record the electrical currents in the human brain.

When electrodes were placed on the surface of the scalp, it caused no pain whatsoever—the person was totally conscious and yet different types of brain waves could be detected. Berger was convinced that these signals were due to psychological energy, which he referred to as P-energy. This was the start of a technique that is still widely used today in neurology: the electroencephalogram (EEG). Contrary to Berger's vision of some special sort of brain/mind energy, the EEG records waves of electricity generated from hundreds of thousands of brain cells just beneath the surface of the brain.

Not only does the EEG show what brain waves look like, but it shows how they vary: the pattern can actually change according to different arousal states. If you are relaxed and conscious, then slow waves will be generated, mainly at the back of your head. This process is called alpha rhythm; you can actually make yourself generate alpha rhythm by relaxing. Increasing numbers of people have problems relaxing, giving rise to one of the greatest scourges of modern times: chronic stress. One way of helping such individuals to learn to relax is to let them know when they are generating alpha rhythm. A particularly ingenious method has involved connecting a person's EEG to a toy electric train, which only actually travels along the track when alpha waves are generated. People can learn to put themselves in the correct state for making the train move. In contrast, if you are excited and aroused, then the pattern of electrical waves changes to one where the neuron is working less as part of a whole group and instead acting more autonomously.

The pattern of EEG can also vary according to age. Electrical activity has been recorded from the mother's womb as early as the third fetal month. It is only in the sixth fetal month that the EEG changes to one of distinct, slow, regular waves. Until children are ten years old, two very slow rhythms can be detected: one is 4 to 7 waves per second ("theta rhythm"); the other is as slow as 1 to 4 per second, but this "delta rhythm" is never seen in healthy, awake adults.

The EEG is important for studying not just normal brain activity but brain disorders as well, such as epilepsy. In epilepsy there is a miniature brain storm of certain groups of brain cells that can lead to convulsions. This virtual explosion of electricity can be detected on an EEG used subsequently by neurologists to locate where damaged brain tissue lies.

Another use of the EEG is to provide a fascinating window into what happens in the brain when we go to sleep. There are four stages of sleep, distinguished by different patterns of electricity recorded from the scalp. When we fall asleep we descend very rapidly from level 1 through these four stages, down to level 4. Throughout the night, we gradually surface and descend again through these four stages.

As well as the four stages of sleep through which we cycle several times a night, there is also another stage of sleep that is totally different. It is in this stage of sleep that our eyes move rapidly backward and forward—hence its name, rapid eye movement or REM sleep. If people are awakened during REM sleep, they usually report that they have been dreaming. It is easy to imagine that the darting eye movements are a result of looking at images that move about in our dream world. Interestingly, during this dreaming state of sleep our EEG is just the same as when we are awake, unlike when we are asleep in dreamless sleep. However, in normal sleep, when we are not dreaming, we might be tossing and turning, but in REM sleep our muscles become paralyzed. This immobility is important because it prevents us from acting out our dreams.

Different animals display different amounts of REM. Reptiles do not display it at all, birds do occasionally, but all mammals, at least according to their EEG, would seem capable of dreaming. In an average night's sleep of some seven and a half hours, humans can spend a total of one and a half to two hours dreaming. The longest recorded single period of continuous REM sleep is about two hours. Given that REM sleep clearly occupies a significant portion of our sleeping time, it presumably has some value. There are several theories on why we dream.

One theory is that since the brain is no longer tied down and restricted by the apparent reality of the messages coming from the outside world, it starts to, in a sense, freewheel. This situation may be analogous to a day off from work with no structure to our activities. However, there must be more to dreaming than the brain just playing around; there is evidence suggesting there is some definite benefit for the dreamer. If people are woken up when their EEG shows that they are in REM sleep, and thus probably dreaming, they try and compensate the following night: the amount of REM sleep that they undergo increases. In one experiment, people were woken up every time their EEG registered REM sleep. They were woken up to ten times on the first night, but by the sixth night they were woken up as many as thirty-three times as their brains tried time and again, in vain, to plunge into the dream world.

Another idea is that dreams enable us to come to terms with problems and consolidate whatever has happened during the day. Although in adults it is easy to see that dreams may have come to serve this purpose, it seems unlikely that it is their prime purpose. The fetus at twenty-six weeks spends all its time in REM sleep, yet has no experiences to consolidate or resolve. Dreaming time then declines gradually through childhood. This observation suggests that dreaming represents more a state of the functioning of an immature brain, where neuronal circuits are still very modest. Perhaps dreaming is a type of consciousness resulting from a less vigorous dialogue between brain regions, caused in turn by the fact that the connecting fibers are still becoming established.

If true, this idea could have two very interesting implications. First, it suggests that when we are in REM sleep, the degree of communication between regions in our brain becomes far less. Second, it has been noted that the consciousness of schizophrenics is frequently very similar to the illogical but very real consciousness of our dreams. Hence it might be the case that a central problem in schizophrenia is a reversal to a reduced communication between regions of neurons, leading to a dreamlike view of the world. Although the function of dreaming might end up being one of consolidation of our problems, it is more likely that dreaming arises as a result of certain states of brain activity that cannot process large amounts of sensory input because we are asleep or because, as in infancy, the brain is underdeveloped, or because, as in schizophrenia, prevailing chemicals have limited the efficacy of large-scale dialogues over large banks of brain cells. Again, however, dreaming is a further facet of consciousness, and thus its cause and its function can still only be extreme conjecture at the most.

But what are the functions of ordinary sleep, when we are completely unconscious? This is an important question because sleep is a pretty risky business—in the Cro-Magnon world into which our species evolved thirty thousand years ago, the sleeper was highly vulnerable to attack from passing predators. Sleep must therefore have some enormous benefit in order to debilitate us in this way for up to eight or so hours per night. It is now known that during sleep the brain makes proteins at a much faster rate than when we are awake. Proteins are large molecules that are essential for maintaining the structure and which underpin the function of all the cells of the body, including neurons. Sleep gives us a chance to stockpile the chemicals that seem to be vital for our brain to function properly. But functioning properly does not refer only to the processes of which we are conscious, such as learning and memory, but to the unconscious processes as well, such as those regulating temperature.

We normally use only a part of the energy derived from food and oxygen for immediate conversion to heat. The remaining energy is stored for all the other vital functions of the brain and body. If people are allowed only three hours of sleep a night, many of these functions start to decline within a week. If we are deprived of sleep, energy is not stored efficiently; more is immediately squandered, dissipated as heat. Thus, persons who are continuously and completely sleep deprived would eventually, literally, be burning themselves out. If rats do not sleep for long periods of time, they gradually need more and more food to restore their energy. Eventually such rats die, underweight and exhausted, despite their huge food intake. Sleep then is vitally important.

Another intriguing feature of the brain and its arousal system is that usually the brain "knows" when to fall asleep. At least in a number of nonhuman animals there is one area of the brain that plays a very important part in sleep and waking: the pineal gland. The pineal gland lies deep at the center of the brain: unlike most other brain structures that are duplicated on each side of a midline, the pineal gland is right over this midline, straddling the middle of the brain.

For this reason the philosopher René Descartes, over three hundred years ago, thought that the pineal gland was actually the seat of the soul. Descartes argued that since there are not two pineal glands and since we have only one soul, the pineal gland must be where the soul is located.

Today we know that the pineal gland is important in regulating sleep and wakefulness. Birds are stimulated directly by light through their skull: we know that even when the pineal gland is isolated from birds completely and put in a dish, it is still sensitive to light. The pineal gland is not responsive when it is already light and becomes dark; however, when it is dark and suddenly becomes light, the cockerel awakens. The pineal gland secretes the hormone melatonin. This substance fluctuates in the brain according to time of day. When levels are high in the brain, sleep ensues; in fact, when melatonin is injected into sparrows they subsequently fall asleep. Although such a simple sequence of events might seem at first glance to be of little relevance to us sophisticated humans, it is worth noting that in the United States melatonin is proving to be a popular treatment for jet lag. A tablet of melatonin taken just before sleep in the new time zone might ensure that sleep occurs rapidly and for a decent period of time.

In humans, the sleep/wake cycle is normally controlled by a variety of factors. We can see just how important these outside clues are from experiments where people have been put in caves and left entirely to their own devices, free from all the demands of the outside world.

David Lafferty, a former Royal Air Force officer, answered an appeal in the *Daily Telegraph* in 1966 for a volunteer to live in isolation in a cave 350 feet underground for at least 100 days. In return he received £100 ($167), plus an additional £5 ($8.35) per day for each subsequent day spent underground. Lafferty set a new record by remaining underground for 130 days. At the end, doctors were surprised at Lafferty's good physical and mental health. Lafferty was surprised when he heard how long he had been underground. His biorhythms had settled into a twenty-five-hour schedule, causing him to underestimate slightly the time he had spent underground. Generally, this modest underestimate seems to occur when people are isolated, so clearly we do have a basic and rather regular internal clock, but we also need to fine-tune it by using cues from the outside world.

Sleeping and waking is not the only rhythm that is controlled by the brain or registered in the brain. There is a very macabre experiment showing a less obvious but important daily rhythm: sensitivity to pain. Amazingly enough, people volunteered to have electric shocks through their teeth at several times throughout the day and night; they then reported on how much pain they felt. It might be expected that these people experienced the same amount of pain all the time. Surprisingly, the pain was perceived as almost twice as bad during certain times of day, most notably in the morning. Just after lunchtime, the pain seemed to be far more bearable.

This study gives us yet another clue as to the functioning of the brain. We can see that experience of pain is a subjective phenomenon, that it can change according to something that is happening within our brain. That event in the brain must, in turn, be changeable. Pain is usually caused by something damaging, or perceived as damaging, that is directly in contact with some part of the body. We saw earlier that signals related to pain were conducted via a specific route up the spinal cord and into the brain. The signals were carried by nerves that did not change their physical properties and hence their efficiency for conduction of electricity did not vary according to the time of day. Some other factor must be at play to account for the diurnal variation.

One of several ways to study pain is to consider the ancient Chinese art of acupuncture. The basic idea of acupuncture is to restore the equilibrium in the functional state of the body so that the so-called life force, "Chi," is in perfect balance between the various organs. The basic procedure involves inserting a needle 1 to 4 millimeters into any one of 365 special points on the body. Acupuncture is used for many purposes—for example, to help people quit smoking. One effect particularly relevant to our discussion is that acupuncture can also relieve pain. An idea as to how the analgesic effects of acupuncture were discovered relates to the time of ancient warfare, when people fought with bows and arrows. As arrows were removed from injured soldiers, they were frequently twisted in the wound, rather as acupuncture needles are today. Paradoxically, the soldiers sometimes experienced a relief from their pain.

The relief of pain from acupuncture can sometimes be so effective that surgery can actually be carried out. To attain a perfect level of analgesia, the needles will have been in place for about twenty minutes. Somehow, acupuncture is interfering with the normal process of sensing pain, whereby nerves in the skin from the affected region send signals to the brain. The analgesic effect of acupuncture is abolished if the nerves in the skin where the needle enters are actually treated with a local anesthetic. It seems that when a nerve is stimulated mechanically by inserting the needle, there is a change in how pain is perceived in the brain. Because the analgesic effect takes some twenty minutes to come on once the needles are in place, and lasts for an hour or so after withdrawing the needles, one possibility is that the needles on their own are not directly responsible, but rather that they must be releasing some natural chemical within the brain, which in turn is able to combat pain. Perhaps it is this chemical that is susceptible to diurnal fluctuations and is even modifiable by drugs.

It was one of the greatest recent discoveries in neuroscience, in the early 1970s, that the brain possesses its own morphinelike substance, enkephalin. When this substance is blocked by drugs, then pain perception increases and acupuncture is less effective. By the same token, morphine mimics this natural chemical, fooling the brain into believing that very high levels of enkephalin have been released. There is no pain center in the brain; rather, enkephalin can be found in a variety of locations within both the brain and spinal cord.

Having failed in Chapter 1 to allocate a function to each particular brain region, we started in this chapter with the reverse strategy: to see how particular functions could be accommodated by the brain. We have seen that in all cases several brain areas are active in parallel to enable us to interact effectively with the outside world. In each description it became obvious that brain electricity and brain chemistry somehow are vital components in the successful functioning, in general, of our sensory, motor, and arousal systems. We have not yet explored just how these forces are harnessed within the brain to transmit the signals that in turn underscore the functions of our daily lives. It is time to explore what brain cells actually are and how they send signals to each other.

....

CHAPTER 3

PULSE, IMPULSE

A great advance in neuroscience took place in an Italian kitchen in 1872. Camillo Golgi (1843–1926), a young medical graduate of Pavia University, was so fascinated by the brain that he had set up a makeshift laboratory. The problem plaguing Golgi concerned the very essence of the physical brain: the matter of which it was composed. At that time, although the brain could be sliced into small slivers and placed under the microscope, only a homogeneous pale mass could be detected. Until its basic building blocks could be identified, it would prove impossible to discover how the brain worked. Then one day, so the story goes, Golgi accidentally knocked a block of brain into a dish containing a solution of silver nitrate, where it remained lost for several weeks. It turned out that Golgi had discovered a critical reaction. When he retrieved the brain block, a transformation had taken place. Under the microscope there appeared to be a complex pattern of dark blobs suspended within netlike tangles. We now know that once brain tissue has been placed in silver nitrate for three hours or more it is possible to visualize the most basic component of brain tissue: the special type of cell referred to as the neuron.

Even more miraculous about Golgi's discovery was that

by a capricious process of which no one is still completely sure, the stain randomly marked out only one cell in every ten to a hundred, so that it appeared black against a pale, amber background. If every neuron had been stained, then the delicate and complex silhouette of the cell would have been buried by overlapping parts of other cells—the whole view of the brain tissue under the microscope would have been transformed into almost uniform blackness. Because only one to ten percent of cells react to the Golgi stain, however, these neurons stand out in stark contrast.

What do neurons actually look like? In all cases there is a squat, blob-shaped region known as the cell body or soma (from the Greek for "body"), measuring some forty thousandths of a millimeter in diameter. Actually, the shape of the soma is usually not as ambiguous and amorphous as a blob, but can come in any one of several characteristic shapes—for example, round, oval, triangular, or even fusiform (shaped like an old-fashioned spindle). It is the cell body that contains all the life-support organs for the neuron, and in this regard neurons are no different from any other cell in the body. However, when neurons are compared to other cells, a very big difference is revealed as soon as one looks beyond the soma. Unlike other cells, there is more to a neuron than just the cell body.

Almost as though it were some kind of microscopic tree, tiny branches grow out of the neuronal cell body. In fact, these parts are named *dendrites,* after the Greek for "tree." The dendrites of a neuron can take on various shapes, vary in density, and emanate from all around the neuron, giving it a starlike appearance; alternatively, they can sprout from one or both ends of the cell body. According to the extent of dendritic ramification, neurons will vary enormously in their overall appearance: there are at least fifty basic shapes for neurons in the brain.

Not only do neurons have these minibranches, but most have a single, long, thin fiber stretching from the cell body.

This fiber is called an axon and it is many times longer than the rest of the neuron. The normal range for diameter of a cell body is some twenty to one hundred thousandths of a millimeter; however, in an extreme case, a fiber such as one running down the human spinal cord can be up to a meter long!

Just by looking at a neuron, it is quite easy to tell the difference between these two special features. Axons are far harder to see, even under a microscope, since they are much thinner than the relatively stubby, branching dendrites. Dendrites are like true branches on a tree in that they taper at the ends, whereas axons do not. The overall appearance of a neuron then is of a squat central region with relatively stubby microbranches protruding and one long, thin strand snaking away. How might such a strange object be the building block of our personalities, hopes, and fears?

Since the cell body contains similar sets of internal apparatus to that of all cells, it is easy to propose that at least some of its functions are to ensure that the cell stays alive and manufactures the appropriate chemicals. However, the role of axons and dendrites is not so obvious, since their very existence is exclusively linked with the specific functioning of neurons alone. Moreover, such clear physical differences between axons and dendrites suggest that they have very different roles to play.

When we saw the power and sensitivity of the electroencephalogram (EEG) in mirroring changing brain states in Chapter 2, we first encountered the idea that neurons can generate electricity. The dendrites act as the receiving area for these signals, like some vast dockland zone receiving goods brought in by a variety of ships. Just as the goods might be unloaded from the docks and dispatched along routes converging on some central factory, so these disparate signals are conducted along the dendrites converging on the cell body where, if the signals are sufficiently strong, a new electrical signal—or to continue the analogy, a new product—will be generated. Then the axons come into play: they conduct this new electrical signal away from the cell body and on toward the next target neuron in the circuit, just as the product of the factory is exported to some faraway destination. In this chapter we will look at how neurons send and receive electrical signals. We will also see how specific chemicals play a very important part in neuronal communication, and how such communication between one neuron and another can be distorted by drugs.

In neuroscience research, this type of approach that starts with a single neuron is referred to as bottom-up. The strategy is to start at the bottom, with the most basic component, the neuron, and then see how communication between one single neuron and another can finally be built into a complex, working whole. The opposite of the bottom-up study is the top-down approach. Here the underlying theme is to start at the top with a macro system, be it a brain region (Chapter 1) or a function (Chapter 2), and see how it might fit into brain operations by traveling down, analyzing it into smaller subsystems. Often, neuroscientists are divided on the repetitive merits of these forms of study. In a sense, we have already been using the top-down strategy in the first two chapters, so we are familiar with its advantages and limitations. In this chapter we turn to the reductionist approach based on the single neuron.

Luigi Galvani (1737–1798) was the first to demonstrate that nerves emanating from the spinal cord could generate electricity. During a thunderstorm, Galvani laid out frog's legs on a metal plate. Surprisingly, the frog's legs twitched as the thunder and lightning resounded. Hence Galvani concluded, wrongly as it turned out, that all electricity lay in living tissue. He envisaged that muscles were containers and nerves were the conductors of electricity. Instead, it was the nineteenth-century pioneering physicist Michael

Faraday who realized how fundamental a phenomenon electricity really was. He concluded from his experiments with nonbiological material that "electricity, whatever its source, is identical in nature." Nerves were indeed a source of electricity, but with no particular monopoly.

An electric current is, literally, the flow of charge. In the brain, such flow will occur due to the movement of any one of four everyday ions (atoms either lacking an electron or possessing an extra one): sodium, potassium, chloride, or calcium. These ions are distributed either inside (potassium) or outside (sodium, calcium, chloride) of the neuron, but they cannot readily enter and leave randomly. Rather, all four ions are kept in one place by a barrier, the membrane of the cell. This membrane is not just a simple wall, but consists of two layers with a fatty middle, like an oily sandwich. Because ions cannot penetrate the oiliness of the inhospitable middle of the membrane of the neuron, no ions will be able to move freely into or out of the neuron.

Consequently, ions amass inside and outside of the neuron. There are also other negatively charged proteins inside the cell. When both ions and proteins are taken into consideration, the net distribution of charge on either side of the neuronal membrane turns out to be uneven; there is not an equal number of pluses and minuses. The inside of the neuron is negative with respect to the outside. There is thus a potential difference—a voltage generated—that is expressed as a negative value and is usually about -70 or -80 thousandths of a volt (mV).

However, there is little point in having this potential difference if the ions remain trapped in one place and are unable to flow, to give rise to a real electric current. Imagine, for example, a dam that has enormous reserves of water stacked up on one side, which you are nonetheless unable to use. For a cell to generate an electrical signal, a current has to flow, just like water has to be unleashed from the dam. In order for the current to flow, the ions need to move temporarily into or out of the neuron. But how is it possible for the ions to travel through the impenetrable oily middle of the membrane?

The membrane barrier can, after all, be breached. Various special structures made from large molecules—proteins—span the two layers of the membrane: they serve as a bridge for a particular ion from one watery, nonoily zone (the outside of the neuron) to another (the interior of the cell). However, since these protein passageways are inserted snugly through the middle of the membrane, a more accurate image is of a tunnel. In conventional neuroscience parlance it is actually referred to as a channel.

For a neuron to send an electrical signal, positively charged sodium ions are briefly able to enter the cell, thus making the potential difference temporarily more positive inside than outside (depolarization). However, as soon as this voltage becomes positive, say to +20 millivolts, positively charged potassium ions then leave the cell, actually making the voltage temporarily more negative than normal (hyperpolarization). Hence, when the neuron is activated in this way, there is a brief and characteristic change in the potential difference, a positive pulse, followed by a negative overshoot. This transient positive-negative wave usually lasts for about one or two thousandths of a second and is known as an action potential. The action potential is distinguished from the voltage (the resting potential) that is normally generated all the time when the cell is not sending a signal. (See Figure 5.)

Why should the sodium channel suddenly open in the first place? To pose the question in another way, What triggers an action potential? After all, it would be completely pointless and almost a paradox to have a signal that was generated completely at random. Imagine the telephone ringing at odd times throughout the night, but there being no caller on the other end of the line. Let us return to the dendrites, the branchlike processes sprouting out of the

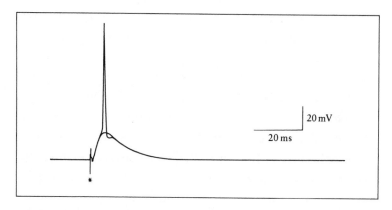

FIGURE 5

Actual recording of a response of a neuron in a rat brain (the hippocampus) to stimulation (shown by an asterisk). Stimulation at this intensity can result either in an EPSP (excitatory postsynaptic potential) or an action potential. In cases of action potential generation, a sharp change in voltage can be seen arising from the peak of EPSP. The action potential is the electrical signal via which neurons communicate. The membrane potential (the potential difference between the inside of the neuron and the outside) becomes transiently more positive (depolarization) as positively charged sodium ions enter the neuron. Once the cell is depolarized, this new voltage causes the opening of potassium channels, allowing positively charged potassium ions to leave the cell (repolarization).

[Courtesy of Fenella Pike,
MRC Anatomical Neuropharmacology Unit, Oxford]

cell body. Dendrites act as receiving stations for incoming signals from other neurons. If the signals are strong and/or sustained, they will be conducted along the branch of the dendrite down to the cell body, like a domestic electric current down a very imperfect leaky cable.

Like some massive and frenetic railway station, tens, hundreds, or even thousands of signals can converge on the central cell body at any one time. This barrage of signals at any one moment will be contributing to its likelihood of generating an electrical signal, an action potential, of its own. As these incoming signals arrive in the cell body they make up one grand super-value, one final change in voltage. If this new net difference in voltage is large enough within the target cell, it causes the sodium channels, which are sensitive to changes to a more positive voltage, to open. Once again a new action potential is generated, this time in the second neuron.

An action potential for any given neuron is always the same size, typically some 90 millivolts. But such consistency poses a problem: If the incoming signals become more numerous or stronger, then how is the receiving neuron, limited to generating only one type of signal, ever going to convey these differences? Because an action potential cannot be made any bigger, the neuron will instead generate more and more action potentials as the signals it receives become more intense. When this happens, a neuron is said to be more excited. The way a neuron signals more or less vigorously is reflected by a change in the frequency of action potential generation. Some neurons can fire up to five hundred action potentials a second (500 Hertz), although it is more normal to record rates of some 30 to 100 Hertz. A neuron that only generates one or two action potentials a second is considered to be slow firing.

Most neurons in the brain will generate action potentials in this way in order to communicate with their respective target cells. The next vital step is for the action potential to reach its intended destination. Just as the dendrites act as the receiving area of the neuron, so the thinner, solitary axon serves as the output path for exporting electrical signals onward. The speed at which the electrical signal—the action potential—is transmitted varies according to the diameter of the axon and whether or not it is insulated with a fatty sheath known as myelin. If the myelin sheath deteriorates, nerve fibers will conduct electrical signals less efficiently, as is the case, for example, in multiple sclerosis. Normal movements are so fast and automatic that it is hard to accept a delay between a thought in the brain and a muscle contraction. The effortless rapidity of our brain processes and our movements can be explained by the speed of nerve conduction, up to approximately 220 miles per hour!

Even though it might be clear how a signal is generated in a neuron and then sent down its axon, it is far from obvious what happens next. We now need to know how one neuron actually makes contact with another, in order to pass on the signal. Ever since nerve cells have been stained and visualized, scientists have pondered this problem. For example, Golgi thought that all neurons were joined together, a bit like a hair net. At the time he was to meet with ferocious opposition from the great Spanish anatomist Ramon y Cajal. These two pioneer neuroscientists polarized into a longstanding conflict because Cajal, contrary to Golgi's vision, was convinced that there was a gap between neurons. The issue was not to be definitively resolved until the 1950s, when there was an awesome breakthrough: the advent of the electron microscope.

The electron microscope enables the study of cells with an astonishing magnification factor. A light microscope, using normal light waves and powerful lenses, can only magnify up to fifteen hundred times; an electron microscope can magnify some ten thousand times. Slices of the brain are coated with a special substance that blocks electrons, and this substance is then absorbed to a different extent by different parts of the neuron. In electron microscopy, a beam of electrons is passed through brain tissue onto photographic film. The more a part of the cell is electron dense, the blacker it appears on film. In electron micrographs, neurons lose their fragile, almost flower-like appearance and instead take on the abstracted beauty of a monochrome form of modern art. Now sturdy black lines and circles form unambiguous patterns not obvious to the untutored eye as parts of axons, dendrites, or soma. But at last, to neuroanatomists at any rate, different parts of the neuron, including its internal machinery, can finally be distinguished. (See Figure 6.)

Once scientists were able to peer at the brain with this degree of accuracy, neurons yielded one of their secrets. The final answer was that Cajal was right: there is indeed a gap—a synapse—between neurons. In the brain, neurons make synaptic contact with each other by the apposition of all manner of different parts of the cell: dendrites can form a synapse with other dendrites, axons with other axons, and axons can make contact directly with the cell body of the target cell. The most common form of synapse occurs when the outgoing part of the cell, the axon, reaches out so that its end point, the axon terminal, makes a synapse with the stubby branching section of the target cell, the dendrite.

The concept of the synapse immediately presents a problem. Just imagine that a signal—an electrical impulse—traveling at some 220 miles per hour, arrives at the end of the axon, and hence at the synapse. True, the end of the axon (the axon terminal) is now excited; the potential is briefly more positive. But where is this wave of excitation going to go? How can it be used as a signal to another neuron when it is stopped short by a gap, the synapse? It is a little like driving in a car and coming to a river; an ideal, albeit extravagant, strategy would be to abandon the car and find a more appropriate means of travel: a boat. We need a way of translating the electrical signal into one that can cross the synapse.

Since the nineteenth century, chemicals have pricked the imagination as being involved, in some way, in neuronal communication. A Frenchman, Claud Barnard, was fascinated by the effects of a poison that is used in South America by Indians when they hunt their prey. Hunters would dip their arrowheads into a substance called curare.

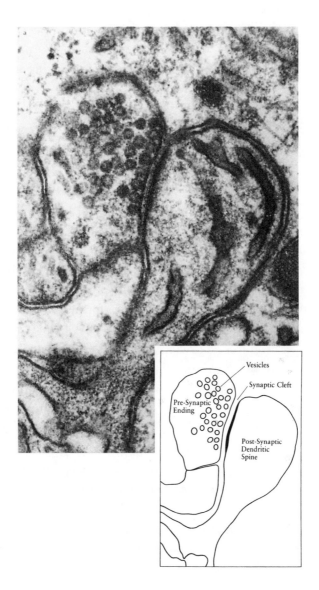

FIGURE 6

An electron micrograph of a synapse (photo). To the left-hand side, a nerve is coming into close contact with the second cell to the right. In the cell on the left are small packets of a transmitter chemical, seen as small circles, that will empty their contents into the narrow gap, the synapse. The areas where the transmitter will diffuse are seen as dark thickenings. A scheme of these two neurons is shown in the inset illustration.

[Adapted from Levitan and Kazmarek, *The Neuron*]

When the arrow embeds into the body of the prey, it does not kill immediately, but paralyzes instead. Barnard suggested that the deadly toxin works by interfering in some way with nerves in the body.

It was not until the beginning of the twentieth century that Barnard was proved right. Curare was discovered to work by blocking a naturally occurring chemical that is released from nerves on to muscles. When you breathe, your diaphragm is operated by a nerve, causing it to move up and down. Obviously, if the signals from this nerve are blocked, your diaphragm will not work and you will be unable to breathe. Hence the lethal effects of the toxin: eventual death through suffocation. A clear demonstration of how this naturally occurring chemical provided the vital link in nerve communication was performed in 1929 by an Austrian, Otto Loewi. The story runs that Loewi acted on an inspiration from a dream he had several nights in a row. His first step was to repeat what was already known: if a nerve that enervates the heart (the vagus) is stimulated, then the heart slows down. It is important to realize that the heart and accompanying nerve on which Loewi was experimenting was no longer in the body. Rather, the organ was kept alive but isolated in a special oxygenated chamber, bathed in a fluid similar to that normally found in the body.

The master stroke of this experiment was that Loewi took the fluid that bathed the original heart and transferred it to a second, unstimulated heart. He found that even though this second heart had not been stimulated, it too slowed down. The only explanation, it seemed, to account for this discovery was that there must be some chemical *released into the fluid* as a result of the stimulation of the first heart. Hence, when the fluid was applied to the second heart, the effects were the same as on the first heart, because the same chemical was present. We now know that this chemical is the one that is blocked by curare: it is a substance called acetylcholine. Acetylcholine is the proto-type of many diverse chemical substances that can be re-leased from diverse nerves and neurons in the brain as the all-important link in the signaling process. They are re-ferred to by the generic term *transmitters.*

This discovery of the action of acetylcholine on the heart was to have profound implications for understanding how brain cells communicate at the synapse. Once we real-ize that electrical stimulation releases a naturally occurring chemical from a nerve, we can see more readily what might happen at a brain synapse, when the end of an axon is effectively stimulated by the electrical signal. As soon as the action potential, the electrical signal, invades the end of the axon, it creates the right conditions by which acetyl-choline is released into the synapse.

At the end of the axon of the signaling cell, within the nerve terminal, acetylcholine is stored in many small pack-ets. As soon as an action potential is propagated down the axon and invades this end region, this transient change in voltage acts as a trigger for some of the packets to empty out their contents—the all-important acetylcholine—into the synapse. The more electrical signals that arrive, the more packets will empty out, and the more acetylcholine will be released. In this way the original electrical signal is converted faithfully into a chemical one: the higher the fre-quency of action potentials, the more acetylcholine re-leased.

Once released, acetylcholine diffuses easily through the watery, salty liquid outside all neurons (the extracellular fluid), crossing the synapse as readily as a boat might cross a river. The time scales are vastly different, however: since such chemicals are relatively small molecules, the synaptic gap is crossed within thousandths of a second. But how does a chemical, a mere molecule such as acetylcholine, actually transmit a message?

Let us return to the car and boat analogy: once the river

is negotiated and we are to continue our journey on dry land, the boat will ideally be relinquished in favor of a car once more. The original electrical signal, which was converted into a chemical one, now needs to be converted back to an electrical impulse. We need to find out how acetylcholine, or any transmitter, might cause a transient change in the electrical status—the voltage—in the target neuron.

Once it reaches the other side of the synapse, each molecule of the transmitter has to make some kind of contact with the target neuron. The transmitter, like a boat, will need to dock. On the outside of the target neuron there are special large molecules, proteins called receptors, that are tailor-made for a specific chemical as precisely as a key is made for a lock or as a hand fits a glove.

A receptor will not just let any old chemical fit into it; it has to be a specific match, where the molecular configuration corresponds perfectly. Once the transmitter is locked into the receptor and bound to it, the creation of a new chemical, a complex of the original two molecules, acts as a trigger for the next series of events to unfold.

The interlocking of the transmitter molecule with the receptor protein on the target cell acts as a molecular starting gun for the opening of channels for sodium, or alternatively one of the other ions. The entry or exit of any of these charged atoms will be reflected in a transient change in potential difference in the target cell. In turn, this change in potential difference becomes just one of the many electrical signals conducted down the dendrites toward the cell body.

In a sense, we have come full cycle. As soon as it arrives at the cell body, this particular electrical signal will contribute, along with tens of thousands of other incoming signals, to a final net change in voltage in the target cell. Once again, if the net change in voltage is sufficiently marked, then sodium channels will open near the cell body, instigating an action potential in this new target cell. Hence the new target cell will itself be sending a signal to become one of thousands impinging on yet the next target cell, and so on in a repeating chain of electrical and chemical events.

Within our brains, there are some hundred billion neurons. To get an idea of just how big a hundred billion is, the Amazon rain forest offers an appropriate analogy. The Amazon rain forest stretches for 2,700,000 square miles and it contains about a hundred billion trees. There are about as many trees as neurons in the brain. But the metaphor need not stop there: if we now consider the huge number of connections between neurons, then we could say that there are about as many as leaves on the trees in the Amazon jungle. It is virtually impossible to imagine on a global scale the fervor of chemical and electrical activity, even if only 10 percent of our hundred billion neurons were signaling at any one moment.

In any case, it is not immediately obvious why the brain should work in this way. After all, it requires a lot of energy to assemble transmitter substances, which requires a complex series of chemical reactions. Furthermore, the chain of electrical-chemical-electrical signaling only works unambiguously if the transmitter is cleared rapidly from the synapse, once it has done its job. Even this process of removal again requires energy either because the transmitter is reabsorbed into the cell that consumes energy, or because the transmitter will be broken down outside of the neuron by energy-consuming enzymes.

Another problem with this system of chemical signaling is time. We have seen that small molecules will diffuse rapidly across the synapse, but the whole process of synaptic transmission takes a few milliseconds. If neurons were fused together and worked just by conducting electrical impulses, then it would be much faster. As it happens, there are some neuron-to-neuron contacts where the neurons appear fused together and there is no need for a chemical synapse. Ironically, Golgi was, at least in these cases, correct after all. In such scenarios no transmitter is used, but the electrical signal is conducted easily and rapidly across these low-resistance contacts (gap junctions). Not only is electrical transmission of this sort much more rapid, but it does not entail the use of energy-consuming chemicals. And yet the majority of synapses in the brain are chemical. Chemical transmission must therefore have enormous benefits to justify, on the face of it, such a squandering of time and energy.

Consider once more how many inputs can form synapses with a target cell: as many as a hundred thousand. In each case, as we have seen, different amounts of transmitter will be released according to the number of action potentials invading the ends of each of the inputs. The activation of the neuron is not fixed but can be *varied* in up to a hundred thousand individual cases. Moreover, by having many different chemicals, each working on its own custom-made target, different transmitters will have different effects on the final voltage. By contrast, electrical transmission will be limited by the passive conduction properties of each neuronal junction. Compared to chemical transmission, electrical transmission, though fast and economical, will be far less variable and diverse. Chemical transmission, on the other hand, endows the brain with enormous versatility: different chemicals have different actions to different extents at different times.

Sometimes a transmitter can be even more subtle in the role it plays in neuronal communication. It can bias how the target cell eventually responds to an incoming message, even though it does not pass on a message. This biasing of neuronal signaling is known as neuromodulation. The concept of neuromodulation, which is relatively recent compared to the now familiar events of synaptic transmission, adds still more power to chemical signaling. Unlike classic synaptic transmission, where we have looked at a single event at some disembodied moment, the idea of biasing the response of a target cell embraces the additional dimension of a particular time frame: first one thing happens, the biasing, then another, the actual signal that will be enhanced or blunted. Neuromodulation complements classic synaptic transmission as a video film might a snapshot. This introduction of a bias for a particular period of time could hardly have been accomplished by the simple passive diffusion of electric current from one cell to the next.

It is this chemical-specific feature of brain function that, in my view at least, makes the brain particularly daunting for those who attempt to model it with computers. If we look at a network of neurons using a high-powered electron microscope, it seems more like some kind of cauldron containing mysterious lumps embedded in masses of vermicelli-like tangles than an integrated circuit board. And yet, the brain has a precision of connectivity of which the circuit board is only a pale echo, as well as the diversity of a chemical factory. *Different* chemicals will be released from different inputs converging on a single cell and active at any moment. In addition, according to the degree of activity of these inputs, different *amounts* of transmitter will be released. Finally, each transmitter will dock into its *own* receptor that has its own characteristic way of influencing the voltage of the target cell. Thus, at every stage there is room for an enormous flexibility and versatility in the brain, using different combinations of transmitter chemicals.

This molecular symphony can hardly be regarded as comparable to the scenario inside a computer. First, and most obviously, the brain is fundamentally a chemical system—even the electricity it generates comes from chemicals. More significantly, beyond the fluxes of ions into and out of the neuron, a wealth of chemical reactions are occurring incessantly in a bustling but closed world inside the cell. These events, some of which determine how the cell will respond to signals in the future, do not have a direct electrical counterpart or any easy analogy with a computer.

Second, the chemical composition of the neurons themselves is changing, and hence there is no separate and unchanging hardware, in contrast to a programmable range of
software. Moreover, the ability for incessant change within
the brain leads to a third distinction from systems in sili-
con: of course, computers can "learn," but few are changing all the time to give novel responses to the same
commands.

True, advanced robotic devices can seemingly organize
and reorganize their own circuits to adapt to certain inputs, but they are still following a set of rules—algorithms—that have been programmed. The brain does not
necessarily operate according to algorithms: What would
be the rule for common sense, for example? The physicist
Niels Bohr once admonished a student, "You are not thinking, you are just being logical." In fact, no external intelligence programs the brain at all: it is proactive, operating
spontaneously when it decides to take its body for a walk
just because it "feels like it." Computers can do some of the
things that brains do, but that does not prove that the two
entities work in a similar way or serve a similar purpose. A
computer that does nothing defies its prime function; a
person who does nothing may well be experiencing a reve-
lation.

Another insight that is generated by looking at the
chemical communication between neurons is to be able to
appreciate why it is so hard to reconcile the top-down and
bottom-up approaches, to extrapolate from an event at the
single synapse, to a function of the brain. The brain is built
up from single neurons in increasingly complex circuits.
These connections are not like a row of people just holding
hands in a line or like the children's game where a message
is passed from one end of a row to the other and ends up
completed distorted. Instead, remember that between ten
thousand and one hundred thousand neurons make con-

tact with any particular neuron. In turn, any particular neuron will become one of many thousands of inputs for the next cell in the network. If we took a piece of brain the size of a match head alone, there could be up to a billion connections on that surface.

Consider just the outer layer of the brain, the cortex. If you counted the connections between neurons in this outer layer at a rate of one connection a second, it would take thirty-two million years! Bear in mind that hominids only evolved seven million years ago, so you would have to count over four times longer than it has taken human beings to evolve. As for the number of different combinations of connections in the cortex alone, it would exceed the number of positively charged particles in the whole universe!

Holistic brain function does not have a simple one-to-one correspondence with any one synapse or class of transmitters. A crude and highly simplistic analogy would be to say that a symphony does not have a direct correspondence with the output of a single trumpet. One way of looking at the brain simultaneously from the top-down and bottom-up perspectives is to consider the action of drugs. We can see how drugs influence behavior while they also change chemical communication at the single synapse. After all, a seemingly individual and unchanging mind is completely at the mercy of our physical brain, our neurons.

Of the many drugs that people take to change how they feel, perhaps the most common is nicotine. Nicotine reaches the brain within ten seconds of the first puff on a cigarette and it is possible to see immediate changes in the smoker's EEG, which becomes desynchronized (see Chapter 2), indicating a less relaxed mode.

Nicotine actually works at one type of receptor—one of the docking areas—that is normally reserved for the transmitter acetylcholine. This action serves as an example of one way in which a drug can work: to mimic the effects of a natural transmitter. However, this mimicry is more of a caricature than an emulation of the normal actions of acetylcholine, for two reasons. First, the amount of stimulation of the receptor is far greater than would normally be the case for acetylcholine itself. Within the brain the repeated and exaggerated stimulation of the receptors for acetylcholine will have long-term effects on brain functioning: the receptors will become less and less sensitive as they are stimulated far more than they would normally be by acetylcholine. Because the target neurons become used to these artificially high levels of chemical, the neurons gradually become habituated: they cannot function normally with normal amounts of acetylcholine. Hence the need for the abnormal amounts of stimulation provided by the drug. This is the chemical basis of addiction.

Second, whereas acetylcholine acts on several different types of receptor, to have more balanced actions, nicotine works on only one receptor type, again resulting in rather one-sided effects. These unbalanced effects will also occur in a more global way outside of the brain: nicotine puts the body into a war mode, ready for fighting or flying. Heart rate and blood pressure increase. Perhaps the feedback to the brain that the smoker is in a flight or fight situation is in itself exciting or pleasurable. Most usually, however, smokers will light up simply because their brain is signaling that its respective receptors need more stimulation.

Another drug that works as a caricature of a natural transmitter, albeit a different one from acetylcholine, is morphine. Morphine is made from a special type of poppy: it is named after the god for sleep, Morphos, because it makes people feel drowsy and relaxed. Heroin is a derivative of morphine, chemically modified so that it is easier to pass into the brain—hence heroin addicts prefer this substance because it enters the brain more readily and thus gives them a quicker effect, a "rush." The side effects of heroin include constriction of the pupils, constipation, and suppression of the coughing reflex. In fact, because of these last two actions it used to be sold as an effective ingredient in anticough and antidiarrhea medications.

A pernicious action of morphine and heroin is to slow down the respiration rate by a direct inhibitory action within the basic part of the brain, the respiratory center in the brain stem, just above the spinal cord, which controls breathing. Sometimes this action can be so severe that breathing stops altogether and the person dies. In fact, inhibition of breathing is the most common acute cause of death in heroin abuse.

Despite its obvious dangers, the clinically most valuable action of morphine is relief from pain. It is the most effective analgesic known, but because of its addictive properties, it is the treatment of choice only to those in very severe or chronic pain, or the terminally ill. A fascinating insight into the nature of pain comes from patients who take morphine: they often say they can feel the pain but it no longer bothers them. Could this action explain why healthy people in no pain still take heroin for "pleasure"? Perhaps, in a similar way, the heroin abuser is no longer bothered by the everyday worries and anxieties of life. This reason for taking heroin soon gives way to another, which is simply to satisfy a craving.

Let us revisit the synapse. The way morphine works is to mimic a certain class of naturally occurring transmitters that we have in our body. Morphine is of a sufficiently similar molecular configuration to fit readily into the receptor protein that is custom-made for these particular transmitters (named enkephalin, endorphin, and dynorphin; see Chapter 2). The drug can thus fool the target neuron that it is being activated by its natural chemical messenger. It was a great discovery in the 1970s that we have these natural agents in our body that work, just as we saw for acetylcholine, to signal between certain neurons. Moreover, at least some of this normal signaling appears in normal situations to be important for relieving pain; for example, if the action of enkephalin is blocked by a certain drug (naloxone), then our perception of pain is worse. Similarly, naloxone prevents at least some of the analgesic effects of acupuncture (see Chapter 2). Mediation of acupuncture analgesia by endorphins would explain the slow onset of the effect, as well as its persistence, even when the needles are withdrawn. Perhaps the acupuncture needles, inserted as they are at critical points, work in part by causing the release of enkephalin and related compounds. (See Figure 7.)

What would be the difference between heroin use and the natural action of enkephalin in the brain? We are not all at risk of becoming drug addicts just because we have a naturally occurring morphine/heroin analogue in our brain. Again, the difference between opioid peptides and

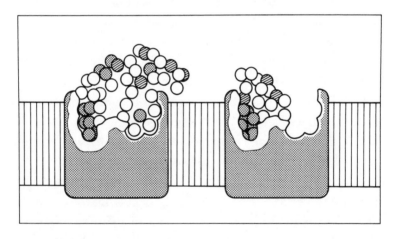

FIGURE 7

The fitting of a chemical transmitter into its own specialized receptor. On the left-hand side a naturally occurring substance in our brain fits perfectly into a special receptor. This interaction will trigger electrical signals within the neuron. Drugs can be made to copy the action of a transmitter by having a similar shape. In this case the drug that has a similar shape to the transmitter enkephalin is morphine.

[Adapted from *The Mind Machine* by C. Blakemore (BBC Books, 1988)]

morphine is comparable to that with acetylcholine and nicotine. Opioid peptides will be released in different places in the brain at different times, and in small amounts. When a drug such as morphine or heroin is taken, however, it will act on all possible brain areas at once, at each and every respective synapse: it will swamp the normal receptor sites. The consequence of such excessive activation of the receptor site is that it becomes accustomed to these higher amounts of chemical and thus far less sensitive to normal amounts. This process of down regulation continues until more and more drug is required to have the same initial effects. Again, addiction is an inevitable consequence.

Another dangerous and addictive drug is cocaine. It is similar to the newer crack cocaine, except that crack is chemically modified so that it can be smoked as opposed to snorted. Cocaine comes from the coca shrub, which grows in the Andes Mountains 1,000 to 3,000 meters above sea level. Nearly 9 million kilograms of these leaves are consumed annually by the 2 million inhabitants of the highlands of Peru, who chew or suck the leaves for the feeling of well-being they produce. Cocaine works on a chemical transmitter in the brain called noradrenaline. Unlike nicotine or morphine, which directly mimic the actions of the transmitters acetylcholine and endorphin respectively, cocaine works in a different way. The drug increases the availability of the naturally occurring chemical itself. Cocaine blocks the process by which noradrenaline is normally removed from the site of action once its role is ended: the drug blocks the transmitter being absorbed into the interior of the neuron, so that it has unnaturally sustained effects.

Cocaine is dangerous because it not only increases the availability of noradrenaline in the brain but also elevates the levels of this transmitter where it works more globally within the body, at the point where the various nerves control vital organs. The effect of noradrenaline is to introduce the body into a false stress situation. Heart rate and blood pressure can increase, thus introducing a risk of stroke. Amphetamine (speed) has a similar effect in that it causes excessive release of noradrenaline and its precursor chemical, the transmitter dopamine. In addition, amphetamine increases the availability of these powerful transmitters even more, by preventing their reabsorption into neurons. Dopamine and noradrenaline are thus active in the synapse for far longer than they should be.

Dopamine, noradrenaline, and even acetylcholine are released from clumps of neurons in the primitive part of the brain (the brain stem) in a fountainlike diffuse arrangement onto the more sophisticated regions of the cortex and immediate subcortical structures (see Chapter 1). These wide-ranging systems of chemical transmitters are related to arousal levels, including sleep and wakefulness. In addition, they can bias, modulate, neuronal activity all over the brain. It is not surprising that drugs that modify these systems will also modify arousal levels. For example, amphetamine users cannot remain still. They cannot concentrate and are incessantly distracted by seemingly neutral objects and events in the external environment. In many regards amphetamine users resemble schizophrenics in that they are constantly at the mercy of the outside world, with no inner resources of mind to assess appropriately what is happening.

A third drug of abuse, ecstasy (3,4-methylenedioxymethamphetamine, MDMA), targets yet a fourth transmitter system (5-HT, also known as serotonin) that also pushes upward and outward from the brain stem. Ecstasy is frequently referred to as a hallucinogen because it gives feelings of disembodiment as well as an overriding feeling of elatedness. This drug causes an excessive release of serotonin. The flooding of the brain with serotonin results in dramatic effects on metabolism, on how temperature is regulated. In addition to feelings of euphoria, the drug causes hyperactivity; it is this incessant and repetitive movement that often characterizes the dancers at raves, where ecstasy is frequently available. A similar effect can actually be seen in rats. A normal rat placed in a box will steadily explore the territory, displaying a variety of different movements, such as rearing, sniffing, walking, and washing. However, when a rat has been given ecstasy, it makes the same movement over and over again, out of the context of its normal behavioral repertoire. This repeated movement is chillingly reminiscent of the type of repeated dancing movements that drug-influenced humans demonstrate.

It is not yet known whether the effects of ecstasy are due to the fact that there has been an explosive release of serotonin, or whether it is the subsequent depletion of the transmitter that has caused the problem. In any event, one serious consideration is that there is now evidence in rats that repeated use of ecstasy over the long term causes death of the clump of neurons (the raphe nuclei) that send a fountainlike spray of axons from the brain stem up and out in a diffuse array to the higher regions of the brain. These neurons are associated with the regulation of a range of very basic functions, including sleep.

These fountainlike serotonin-releasing neurons are also the target for much antidepressant medication. Many antidepressants act by enhancing the availability of serotonin, albeit by a different mechanism and in a way that does not result in the neurons being killed. The most popular antidepressant to date, Prozac, works in this way. However, if a net increased availability of serotonin is associated with "happiness," it follows that taking a drug such as ecstasy that enhances release of serotonin in the short term will have a similar effect. If, unlike antidepressants, repeated use of ecstasy leads to death of the nerve endings, and thus permanent depletion of serotonin, then sustained use of ecstasy would be predicted to have a depressant side effect.

In fact, there is some data suggesting that long-term use of ecstasy can be followed by depression and suicide.

We can see that drugs affect the brain in many ways due to the variety of brain chemicals upon which they act and the different stages in synaptic transmission at which they intervene. Nicotine and morphine mimic a particular, naturally occurring compound by acting at its receptor, whereas cocaine increases the availability of another type of substance, before it diffuses across the synapse. Ecstasy is different in that it actually depletes the brain of yet a third type of transmitter chemical. Because we have so many transmitter chemicals in our brain, there are highly specific targets as well as these highly diverse ways in which drugs can act. We know to a certain extent what drugs can do, but we do not really know the full effects in the long term or the side effects on the rest of the body.

Perhaps the most tantalizing issue is the link between the known molecular/cellular change and the change in the way we actually feel. Why should overstimulation of enkephalin receptors by morphine actually give rise to the subjective sensation of euphoria and a disregard for pain? How might antidepressants work at the level of the synapse such that enhanced availability of serotonin leads to an alleviation of depression? This conundrum is particularly stark if we bear in mind that antidepressants are biochemically effective within hours but therapeutically take some ten days to work. There is obviously no simple one-to-one relation between a single class of molecule and a particular mood.

In this way, consideration of the action of drugs highlights the still elusive nature of the link between specific and well-defined events at the synapse and how those synaptic events actually constitute an emotion. One of the greatest challenges of neuroscience is to explain how the top-down phenomenon of, say, happiness, can be explained by the bottom-up building blocks of synaptic transmission and chemical modulation. It is truly tantalizing to imagine how our unique consciousness is really at the mercy of a cocktail of brain soup and spark. The issues of how a unique, individual brain is assembled, and how it is expressed, are tackled respectively in the next two chapters.

CHAPTER 4

....

CELLS UPON CELLS

Someone once asked the physicist Michael Faraday, "What use is electricity?" He replied, "What use is a newborn babe?" It is easy to take Faraday's point: human babies seem particularly helpless. It takes us some sixteen years to realize our potential as adults, whereas a rat born within twenty-six days of conception takes only two months or so to become fully mature. An elephant spends over twice as long in the womb as we do, some twenty to twenty-two months, but is then mature within eleven years. So why do we serve, by comparison with other animals, such a long apprenticeship for life? In 1883, the philosopher and historian John Fiske, who popularized evolutionary theory in the United States, asked, "What is the meaning of infancy? What is the meaning of the fact that man is born into the world more helpless than any other creature, and needs for a much longer season than any other living thing, the tender care and wise council of his elders?" We shall explore this question as we look at the development of the brain and identify the factors that make an individual.

Life starts with the fertilization of the mother's egg, when a single sperm from the father burrows into it. This act induces chemical changes that preclude the entry of any further sperm from within the multitude thronging and

93

amassing around the egg. But it is a long way from an egg with a diameter of about 0.005 inches to a brain. The first step toward building a brain, and indeed the rest of a body, is to form a single cell from the egg and the sperm: a zygote. After just over a day, some thirty hours, this zygote divides into two cells and repeats the process again and again so that within three days it has formed into a ball of cells resembling a mulberry, hence its name *morula* (Latin for "mulberry").

Five days following fertilization, the cells within the morula split into two groups. One group forms an outer wall, creating a hollow sphere, while the remaining cells congregate into a tight inner mass within the sphere at one end. The morula is now a blastocyst; the cells making up its outer wall will provide nourishment for the developing embryo, which will be created from the inner cell mass. However, it is still only six days after conception. The next vital stage is for the blastocyst to become implanted in the lining of the womb, whereby the new life will have access to all the nutrients it will need for the next thirty-nine weeks or so.

Within about a day of implantation, the inner ball of cells that had congregated within the blastocyst has separated from the outer wall where it fuses with the womb. This jumbled mass of cells has started to flatten into the embryonic disk, an oval sheet that is two cell layers thick. It is incredible to contemplate that this thin little disk is the ultimate source of all the different cells that will make up the human body, but already these early pioneers have started to diversify, albeit rather crudely.

At around twelve days, certain cells in the upper layer of the disk start to move toward the middle, as though in some rehearsed and choreographed dance. In the middle of the embryonic disk these mobile cells then insert themselves between the original upper and lower layers, threading along the disk and thus creating a third layer of cells.

The embryonic disk is now three layers thick. It is at this stage that we can first focus on the future brain. The middle layer of cells appears to send chemical signals to the upper layer of cells so that they will diversify again, to become neurons. Embryologists refer to this upper layer of precursor neurons as the neural plate.

By about eighteen to twenty days the neural plate starts to change in the middle, in that the center sinks inward and the edges move upward and out. After three weeks, these edges will start to rise up, creating a neural groove. The edges of the groove then fold inward and fuse so that they form a kind of cylinder, a neural tube. By the end of the first month in the womb, a primitive brain has already been formed. In fact, well before the neural tube took shape, the young brain was starting to manifest itself. Even at the stage of the neural plate, certain segments were already destined to form specific brain regions.

By the fifth week in the womb it is possible to identify two bulges at the front that are the foundation of our hugely developed cerebral hemispheres, as well as certain regions below the cortex such as the basal ganglia, which we saw in Chapter 2 were important for movement. Encasing all this turbulent, burgeoning activity is the skull. The developing skull has membranous regions to enable it to expand and thus allow for this frantic growth; it is only much later in life, when the brain has reached full size, that the bone can finally become fused together.

The neurons-to-be will divide several times each, so that there is a massive proliferation in cell number: at maximum rates, cells will be dividing to give 250,000 new neurons per minute! The primitive brain continues its development as the top of the neural tube thickens into three swellings. By the start of the second month, there are recognizable brain regions in place. The front stump of the neural tube initially bends in two places set almost at right angles with the developing spinal cord, as parts of the brain grow faster than others. The very front part swells into two hemi-spheres; at around eleven weeks, the back part sprouts an outgrowth that becomes the easily recognized little brain, the cerebellum.

It is due to the closed neural tube that cavities in the brain—ventricles—are formed. These ventricles constitute an interconnecting labyrinth that finally opens onto the spinal cord, and through which pores allow for the circula-tion of the colorless fluid that is going to bathe the entire brain and spinal cord for life. It is this cerebrospinal fluid that the philosopher Galen (see Chapter 1) had thought many centuries ago was the "psychic pneuma," the seat of the soul, and which is sampled nowadays in the routine di-agnostic procedure of lumbar puncture.

In the nineteenth century it was a popular idea that the development of the human brain reflected development in evolution: according to this idea, our brain in the womb would first resemble that of a reptile, then that of a fish, then a bird, and finally lower mammals such as a rat, via cats and the like, to higher mammals. Toward the end of gestation, the brain would be similar to that of the foremost group of animals, literally the primates, from which des-tiny led ultimately to humans. Even into the first half of the twentieth century, such thinking continued: in one of his novels, Aldous Huxley refers to the "ex-fish" standing in his bishop's robes and proffering his bishop's ring.

However interesting and attractive this idea might be that ontogeny (individual development) reflects phylogeny (species development), it is not really valid as a blanket generalization. One brain is not simply more developed than that of some "lower" species. Evolution is more like a bush than a ladder, with species developing along different lines according to the dictates and needs of particular lifestyles. At no time does a human fetal brain resemble, for example, that of a snake, where the regions associated with smell (olfactory tubercle) are particularly well developed. Rather, each brain has evolved for the individual lifestyle of a particular species. The human cerebellum at no time in development occupies either a half or 90 percent of total brain mass, as is the case for the cockerel and certain fish, respectively. The cerebellum is a structure that is the least changed across species; however, it is the high proportion of brain mass devoted to cerebellum that is a departure from the basic ground plan, the variation on the theme that fits a particular species. Presumably, the lifestyles of the fish and the cockerel, compared to the human, are dominated much more by the need to generate movements that are exquisitely coordinated with the incoming senses. A disproportionately large cerebellum is not a statutory rite of passage for developing brains of all species.

On the other hand, a striking feature of the developing human brain is how the immature cortex at different stages does indeed resemble that of others species. The cortex of rats, rabbits, and guinea pigs, for example, is smooth in texture, whereas that of the cat has some convolutions. By the time we arrive at the primate brain, these convolutions have increased markedly, while the surface of the mature human cortex resembles a walnut. Interestingly enough, these convolutions appear only relatively late in the development of the human brain, at about seven months' gestation. The advantage of a folded cortex is that more surface area can be accommodated in a restricted space. Imagine scrunching up paper into a bin: the more crumpled the paper, the more can be accommodated.

In this case it would seem that the development of a wrinkled cortex was a case where ontogeny did reflect phylogeny. But perhaps the function of the cortex can be directly related to the general sophistication of the brain, irrespective of species-specific peculiarities in lifestyle. If the cortex is the most important area for cognitive processes, as suggested in Chapter 1, then clearly the more cortex one has, the better for being as flexible and adaptable to one's particular environment as possible.

On the other hand, dolphins have more convolutions on their cortex than we do, yet are estimated to be only as intelligent as dogs. Size of cortex, and hence the number of convolutions, is not the only determining feature. Dolphins have large brains simply because the size is not constrained, as it is with humans, by the pelvic bones of the mother. Although dolphins might have a large surface area of cortex, it is thinner than that of humans and the neurons within are organized in a less complex pattern. Thus, convolutions of the cortex are clearly a factor in determining the eventual power of the brain, and increase as we grow in the womb and during evolution, but other factors are important as well.

For all species, the sequence of events in growing a brain at the level of the basic building blocks, the neurons, is the same. If the brain is to grow and if the brain is made of neurons, then those neurons must continue to increase in number. The cells destined to be neurons meet the demands of the developing brain by splitting themselves in two. In order to divide, a neuron precursor will embark on a short journey that can be recycled several times. By putting out a tentacle-like extension, the central mass of a neuron slithers from the outer region of the neural tube toward the center. Once at the center, the nucleus will divide so that the two new cells then push back to the outer edge of the neural tube to start the cycle again.

It is important to remember that the brain is not just a homogeneous mass, but, as we saw in Chapters 1 and 2, it is composed of highly specialized regions that can be distinguished by shape and by the operations they perform in overall brain function. It is not only vital for a growing brain to have more cells but to have them in the right regions. A neuron, then, once it has undergone several cycles of division, must migrate to its correct location in the new brain.

Initially, neurons will simply migrate from the outer to the inner region of the neural tube, but as this zone becomes thick with cells and well established, cells will move in different directions according to their different destinies. For example, some cells that move just below this middle region are going to become a special type of neuron—interneuron—that connects other neurons in small, local circuits. Alternatively, some of the cells that move to this region will become glial cells.

Glial cells are not neurons at all but they abound in the brain, where they actually outnumber neurons ten to one. The term *glia* derives from the Greek for "glue." When these cells were first observed they had the appearance of sticking to neurons. There are various types of glial cells with different functions. One glial type (macrophages) plays a part in removing the debris of dead cells within the brain following damage; another class of glial cells generates a fatty sheath around many neurons to act as electrical insulation.

The type of glial cell that is named after its starlike shape, astrocyte, and that is the most ubiquitous does not appear to have any single role. Originally, astrocytes were thought to have a rather passive function, preventing the neuron from slithering around by providing a type of biological netting, known more formally as the extracellular matrix. It is now clear, however, that astrocytes play a wide range of diverse and more dynamic roles. In the healthy adult, these non-neuronal cells protect neurons by ensuring that the microenvironment around the neuron remains benign in its chemical composition. They act as a type of sponge or buffer for mopping up potentially excessive or toxic amounts of chemicals. In the event of actual neuronal damage, astrocytes will redouble their efforts and increase in size and number so that they can release high levels of substances to enable subsequent neuron growth and repair of the injury.

How might glial cells be important in migration of neurons to the far corners of the developing brain? Although neuronal migration is a long way from being well understood, it is known that one particularly important job of glial cells in the development of the brain is to act as a kind of temporary scaffolding. Glial cells set off from their point of origin ahead of neurons, as though laying a track. In their wake, the neurons then slither along the glial cells as though on a kind of monorail. If the glia are absent, then certain neurons will not be able to migrate, with dire consequences.

One of the best-known illustrations of the type of problems that ensue when neurons in the brain are unable to migrate along their glial monorail occurs in a certain strain of mutant mouse, the weaver, so named because of the severe disorder of movement displayed. Instead of walking in straight lines, these mice will suddenly turn in random directions, and are generally weak and subject to incessant trembling. The problem for the weaver mouse lies in the little brain at the back of its head, the cerebellum. Due to a mutation in the genes, the glial cells in this region do not develop as they should, resulting in a class of cerebellar neurons that do not migrate to their rightful place. In turn, further neurons end up misaligned and the whole cerebellum remains abnormally small. As we saw in Chapter 2, since the cerebellum is important in coordinating movement and senses, it is hardly surprising that animals with such a compromised cerebellum exhibit disorders of movement. At the moment it is a mystery how each neuron knows when to get off the monorail, to alight in its particular place in the future brain.

As more and more neurons proliferate, migrating along the glial monorail and then alighting, gradually the brain is growing, accumulating cells layer upon layer a little like an onion. Eventually, the outermost layer, the cortex, starts to assemble from an initial thin layer of cells, the cortical plate. As more cells arrive, they have to journey through this first layer of new cortex to form a second layer, and so on. In the mature cortex, there are six layers in all. The neurons that were the first to arrive during development constitute what ends up as the deepest layer of cortex, that furthest from the outer brain surface; the neurons in the outermost layer of cortex, forming the very surface of the brain, were the last to migrate.

What makes a cell become a cortical neuron? Again, as with the actual point of descent from the glial monorail, little is known of this means of neuronal specification. We do know that in the brain there are molecules known as cell adhesion molecules that may act a little like sticky badges, so that it is easy for neurons literally to stick together to form a group. For example, there are certain experiments where individual cells from different parts of the developing retina have been removed and mixed together with other neurons from other populations of potential brain regions; the original cells taken from the retina tend to retain their specification in that they can find each other and reaggregate. The commitment of any neuron to a particular size, shape, location, and connectivity will be occurring at different times. In addition, it is likely that the chemical that a cell will use as its transmitter is determined once and for all as soon as the neurons have stopped proliferating. By nine months' gestation, we have most of the neurons in our brains that we are ever likely to have. (See Figure 8.)

So now we are born! Birth allows the brain to go on growing, since otherwise the head would soon become too big for the birth canal of the mother. At birth, the human head is roughly the same size as a chimpanzee, some 350 cubic centimeters. By six months, it will be half its eventual size, and by two years it will be three quarters the size of the adult head. At four years old the human brain is four times the size it was at birth, some 1,400 cubic centimeters.

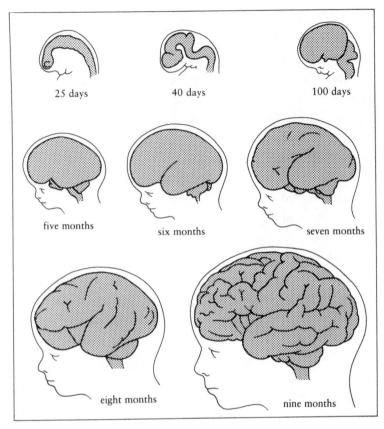

FIGURE 8

The developing human brain.

[Adapted from M. Cowan,
Scientific American (September 1979)]

Even within the first month of life, a baby already has some reflexes. A reflex, as we saw in Chapter 2, is an unchanging response to a given, fixed situation. One such reflex is a scooping movement of the arm that will underlie the eventual sophisticated ability to grasp objects. This reflex is seen if one tries to pull the baby's upper arm away from his body: the baby's response is to retract his arm, bringing it back into his trunk. This grasping reflex becomes more and more refined as the months pass. From curling all his fingers around an object placed directly in the palm, the baby becomes able to turn his hand to grasp an object brought into contact with the back of his hand. Finally, he is able to perform voluntary grasping, where he is first able to reach of his own accord for whatever is in view.

These stages of the development of grasping parallel changes occurring in the baby's cortex. During the first months of life there is a massive increase in the cortex in the insulating substance myelin (see Chapter 3). Once the axon is insulated with myelin, it conducts the electrical signal far more efficiently. Clearly, a movement as delicate as voluntary reaching can only occur when the neurons in the cortex are working as efficiently as possible. Myelination continues apace right up to fifteen years of age, and even beyond. Furthermore, it is a pleasing thought that myelin can even continue to increase in density to as late in life as sixty years of age.

The ultimate skill in picking up objects comes, often unnoticed, toward the end of the first year of life. Whereas young babies can only move all digits simultaneously, the older child becomes able to move his fingers independently. In particular, the pincer movement is now possible, where a small object is picked up with the thumb and forefinger. The main group of animals able to make these types of movements is the primates. Unlike many other species, such as the cat or dog, there is a direct connection in primates from the area of cortex directly associated with control of movement (the motor cortex, see Chapter 2) right on to the immediate nerves in the spinal cord that are responsible for contraction of muscles in each digit.

It is this fine finger movement that is the most refined, the most advanced. Within the motor cortex it is the digits that have some of the largest allocations of neurons. Moreover, when the motor cortex is damaged, it is the fine finger movement that frequently does not reappear, even though most other movements miraculously return.

Once able to move each finger independently of the others, manual skills increase enormously. This improved manual dexterity means that tool making is far easier, which in turn will help enhance the progress and survival of the species. On the other hand, independent digit movement on its own is not the secret to the sophistication and versatility of the primate lifestyle. The hamster and racoon also have good control of their digits.

Not all reflexes in babyhood serve as precursors to voluntary patterns of movement. Babinski sign, named after the man who first reported it, disappears in infancy. If the balls of the feet in an adult are stroked, then the toes tend to curl inward, after a one-second delay. However, in babies this stroking of the balls of the feet results in the toes being flexed upward in a fanning movement. As with the grasping reflex, changes in the Babinski reflex during development reflect a changing nervous system. The Babinski sign changes as soon as neurons in the motor cortex (see Chapter 2) become properly connected with the neurons in the spinal cord that control muscle contraction. In normal, mature nervous systems, the motor cortex sends impulses down the spinal cord to cause contraction of the muscle, seen as a curling of the toes—hence the short delay of a second in which the input of the stroking is transmitted up the spinal cord to the brain, processed, and then sent back down the spinal cord. Since the curling of the toes in response to stroking the ball of the foot requires the integrity of certain parts of the brain and the ascending and descending spinal tracts, this test is also used for diagnosis in adults with suspected damage to the spinal cord or brain. If certain parts of the brain or the descending spinal tracts are damaged, then the positive Babinski sign will re-emerge, the local circuitry in the foot will predominate, and the adult will revert to the reflex of the baby and fan out his or her toes.

Some reflexes disappear altogether; for example, if supported and held with their feet touching a surface, very young babies will make walking movements. No one really knows the point of this walking reflex. There was once an idea that the more a child was able to practice the walking reflex, the more efficient and more quickly it would learn to walk. It is now known that this is not true.

It is not just our voluntary functions, such as grasping and walking, that gradually develop after birth. Another system for involuntary functions has also come into play. We know that the brain is processing information from the outside world, enabling the body to move about in its particular lifestyle. The brain receives signals not just from the outside world but also from the body. These internal signals are bombarding the brain incessantly, although we are for the most part oblivious to what is happening. We do not, for example, continuously and deliberately have to control our breathing, heart rate, or blood pressure; such repetitive and tedious tasks would leave us no time for any other activity, including sleep.

Because communication to and from the brain to our vital organs seems to work mostly of its own accord, it is referred to as the autonomic nervous system. The autonomic nervous system is under direction from the brain, but physically extends beyond it, in that it comprises sets of nerves emanating from the spinal cord that are in contact with all our vital organs. These nerves have developed separately from the central nervous system, the brain and spinal cord, at a very early stage in gestation. As the neural plate is closing to form the neural tube at about three weeks after conception, a small group of would-be neurons on either side is not included. These cell groups are referred to as the neural crest and they will give rise to the nerves that make up the autonomic nervous system.

The autonomic nervous system is not just some sort of steady-state mechanism but actually has two modes in which it works: a war mode and a peace mode. When a loud noise surprises you, your heart rate increases auto-matically. The survival value for an increased heart rate is that your body is preparing for an emergency action where you might have to exert yourself by running or fighting, and therefore your blood is pumping much more quickly to give you more oxygen. This is war mode, properly referred to as sympathetic division of the autonomic nervous sys-tem. The sympathetic division is activated when the usual daily activities, which are not necessary for immediate sur-vival, are suspended. In this condition, you need sweat to cool down, there is no time for digestion, and the blood carrying oxygen is needed in vital organs, so that your heart rate and blood pressure go up; airways are dilated so that you can breathe more easily and an organ known as the adrenal medulla releases adrenaline to circulate around the body to help keep the organs responding appro-priately.

Nowadays we are not necessarily hunting or being hunted in a literal sense; however, when you feel nervous or excited, your body has all the atavistic reactions needed on the early Cro-Magnon savannah. Your sympathetic ner-vous system operates as though you are going to fight or flee, even if you do not actually do anything. As you pick up the phone to hear the result of an exam, job interview, or medical test, you might sense your heart thud and you might feel hot and a little sweaty, especially in the palms of your hands. It is this response of sweaty palms that can change the ability of the skin to conduct electricity and thus be detected as a changing signal with lie detection ma-chines.

Peace mode, known as the parasympathetic division, is the default condition and operates when we do not need to place immediate survival as the top priority. We have time to relax and to digest food without being on red alert to re-spond to a rapidly changing situation. The heart rate is slow and steady and food is being steadily digested; we do not need sweat to cool down or dilated airways to maximize breathing.

Although it is normally the brain that controls the vital organs, the state of the body can also feed back to influence the state of the brain. For example, a certain drug such as propranolol (a "beta-blocker") that slows down the heart rate does not itself gain access to the brain. Nonetheless, this drug can be taken as a calming agent simply because the slowed heart rate, rather like deep breaths, registers in the brain that a nonstress situation prevails—that is, the parasympathetic nervous system is at work.

The reflex responses of the autonomic nervous system can also include adaptations to situations that are more specific to certain organs, rather than the global conditions of being on red alert or being relaxed. One reflex that everyone can observe is the response of the iris to light. We know that when a light is bright, the pupil automatically constricts, and dilates again when the light is dim, thus ensuring the correct amount of light is let into the eye. The iris also responds automatically to emotion. If we are admiring something or feeling affectionate and tender, then our pupils automatically dilate. Apparently some wily salespeople have trained themselves to observe a customer's eyes to assess the chances of a potential sale. Moreover, dilation of the pupils is considered a feature in enhancing attractiveness.

In a well-known, classic experiment, male subjects were asked to sort photographs into one of two piles according to whether the females in the photographs were attractive or not. There were many photographs, so the subjects would have been unable to remember individual faces. The result was that they frequently put duplicate photographs of the same woman onto different piles. The only difference was that in one case the pupils of the women had been touched up to look as though they were dilated. The men were subconsciously registering dilated pupils as the decisive factor in assessing attractiveness. In the nineteenth century, women contrived this reflex by taking a drug that blocked a certain type of receptor to the transmitter acetylcholine (see Chapter 3); hence the colloquial name of the drug (atropine), *bella donna,* meaning "beautiful lady."

And so we are born equipped to adapt to stress and with a certain number of reflexes. But are we conscious? This perplexing question has never been satisfactorily answered. All the possibilities seem bizarre. One scenario is that we are conscious in the womb, but then the problem arises of identifying exactly when this momentous event occurs. Clearly, the single fertilized egg is not conscious, so when would consciousness suddenly intervene? And of what could a fetus be conscious? Another idea might be that the baby becomes conscious precisely as it is born. Again, this is a strange idea as many babies are born prematurely. So is it the act of birth itself that evokes consciousness? It seems hard to accept this line of thought as the brain itself is completely unaffected by the birth process.

An alternative idea is that the child may become conscious sometime after birth. Not only would this scenario imply that the neonate was merely an automaton but the problem is again posed of identifying the critical stage when consciousness occurred. The development of the brain in both the fetus and the neonate is a gradual process. It is therefore impossible to identify some distinct and conspicuous event that could be correlated with the onset of consciousness.

There is another possibility. Since the brain develops slowly and gradually, perhaps consciousness does also. It could be the case that consciousness is not an all-or-none phenomenon, but that it grows as brains do. If we accepted that consciousness were a continuum in this way, then it would follow that the fetus is conscious, but conscious to a far lesser degree than the human adult, or even the human newborn. This way of looking at consciousness would also help with regard to the riddle of whether nonhuman animals were conscious. The less sophisticated the brain, the less the degree of consciousness. Hence, animals would be conscious, but a chimpanzee would be conscious to a lesser degree than its human counterpart, as the brains of the two species, so similar at birth, then follow different fates.

The brain of the human and that of the chimpanzee are of comparable weights at birth. A vital difference is that the primate brain, including that of the chimpanzee, undergoes most of its development within the womb. For the human, much of its development—some might say most—occurs outside the womb. Might this postnatal growth of the brain give us any advantages over our chimpanzee cousins, who differ from us by only 1 percent of their DNA (deoxyribonucleic acid)?

Our brain, and its process of development in the womb, has been the same for thirty thousand years. With the brains we have as newborn babies we could have just as easily been ushered into the world of early Cro-Magnon man. Stated another way, the brain of an early Cro-Magnon baby could have been as intellectually agile and comfortable with computers as are many young people in developed countries today. The critical challenge for the adaptable and impressionable young human brain is to develop and mature under the particular stimulation and constraints of the environment in which it is going to have to survive, whether it is one of jungles or computers. Unlike our chimpanzee relatives, our brains have an extraordinary capacity to adapt to the environment in which we are placed. Judging from the astonishing rates of growth of the newborn human brain, and the parallel development of behavior, it is clearly operating on a very tight schedule.

By nine months after conception, most of the neurons

that will constitute our brain have proliferated to the appropriate brain region. Once at their destination, each neuron effectively sets down roots and initiates communications with neighboring neurons by establishing a synaptic circuitry (see Chapter 3). All the time in the new brain, the axons are now growing out from the neurons to connect them to other neurons. Much of the spectacular increase in brain size after birth is actually attributable to the development of these processes acting as lines of communication between neurons, rather than simply to the addition of more neurons. (See Figure 9.)

Even when grown in a dish—in tissue culture—brain cells will send out their axons. Therefore, using a time-

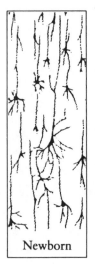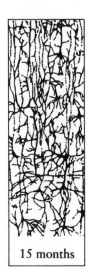

| Newborn | 3 months | 15 months | 2 years |

FIGURE 9

The development of the human cortex is characterized by an increase in the number of connections. Although individual cells can be readily seen in the newborn cortex, by two years the neurons are hard to discern in a dense network of connections.

[From *The Post-Natal Development of the Human Cerebral Cortex* Vol. 1 by J. L. Conel (Cambridge: Harvard University Press, 1939)]

lapse video, it is possible to observe directly brain cells reaching out to their neighbors to establish contact. Viewed in this way, it is hard not to anthropomorphize the developing cells. As they move on film, they appear highly purposeful, yet with the fragility of spun sugar, moving across the screen with alarming speed while almost literally feeling their way by means of fluted, weblike endings that undulate and flutter as they make their inexorable progress. Almost a century ago Ramon y Cajal (see Chapter 3) referred to these endings of the nerves by the highly apposite term *battering rams;* however, their scientific name is growth cones. When looking at such films, it is hard to understand how anyone could view the brain as a computer or even compare it with one.

How do these young neurons know where to go? It is thought that their primary orientation is probably genetic, but that any final routing will be fine-tuned later by local factors. Another idea is that the target cells release a guiding chemical. The concentration of this chemical will be strongest near the target and weaker as it diffuses away. By moving in the direction where the concentration of the guiding chemical becomes stronger, the axon would finally arrive at the target.

The prototype chemical identified as important in controlling the growth of nerves is nerve growth factor (NGF). It is thought that NGF works primarily by being carried back inside a cell once contact between neurons has been established. Once transported back in this way, NGF possibly invades the nucleus to interfere with the expression of genes, in that it switches off a genetically programmed self-destruct mechanism. Conversely, if antibodies to NGF are given, then the neurons in which it normally operates will die. But brain development does not rely exclusively on NGF. While NGF is used in neurons outside of the brain and on certain neurons within the brain, it is only one example of many such probable guiding chemicals.

It is hard to imagine how such processes would work for some of the very long distances that axons are known to travel. A further possibility, during early development when the brain structures are still close, is that there are a few pioneer fibers that then become stretched out like melting toffee, but along which other axons will be able to follow.

In any event, it is certain that these growing axons are not irrefutably fixed in their course. Rather, growing neurons can adapt sensitively to changing circumstances to make the best of a situation; for example, if the outgrowing axons are reduced, or the intended target is partially destroyed. Such scenarios have been demonstrated in relatively simple systems that are tractable to experimental manipulation and where it is already known that the outgrowing neurons form an orderly one-to-one connection with their target.

In the frog's eye, for instance, each axon leaving the eye has a particular target territory that it will invade within the relevant target structure (the tectum) in the frog's brain. If a neuron is coming from the extreme right of the eye, it will invade territory in the extreme right of the tectum. The next neuron, just to the left of the first cell, will occupy target territory just to the left of that of the first cell, and so on. This type of organization is referred to as topographical. The topographical connections of neurons can be so precise that even if the eye is rotated 180 degrees, the axons will still grow into their intended patch, with devastating results. Any frog so modified will now see the world upside-down and thus will have enormous trouble catching flies.

However, a topographical arrangement of neurons can adapt to extract the best from a changing situation. If half the outgrowing neurons are destroyed, then the remaining 50 percent of neurons—which would in normal circumstances have occupied respectively only 50 percent of the tectum—will now invade the entire territory. Conversely, if half of the tectum is destroyed, then the full complement of outgrowing neurons will crowd into the smaller target space, but still in a topographical manner: they will thus each have half as much target territory as normal.

Another way we can appreciate the adaptability of neurons is by looking at a part of the body that is very important to animals: whiskers. Whiskers allow animals to pass through narrow openings. As soon as they are touched, the whiskers, which are the same width as the widest part of an animal's body, send signals via nerves to the brain. If the whiskers are touched simultaneously on both sides, it is clear that the animal's head is in contact with a passage that will be too narrow for the rest of its body to enter.

Whiskers are served by nerves that project into the brain, where they are allocated neurons that are grouped together in arrangements that resemble the silhouette of a barrel. These neuronal barrels can be seen easily, even under the light microscope. It is relatively straightforward to tamper experimentally with this particular neuron-to-target relationship by extirpating some of the whiskers. In the mouse brain we can see an adapting situation comparable to that in the frog's brain. If the system was rigidly programmed and inaccessible to change, then one would expect to see conspicuous gaps in the barrel-like organization of neurons in the brain. These gaps would presumably occur because it was no longer necessary to have neurons allocated to whiskers that had been pulled out. In reality, just as we saw for the frog, all target territory still ends up being used: there are much larger groups of neurons allocated to the remaining neurons. The barrels of neurons become enlarged to fill the available space.

Although this experiment might have little relevance for humans at first glance, a similar chain of events caused a tragedy for a young Italian boy. This six-year-old was blind in one eye. The cause of his blindness was a medical mystery. As far as the ophthalmologists could tell, his eye was totally normal. Eventually, the enigma was solved. It finally emerged that when he was a baby, the boy's eye was bandaged for two weeks as part of the treatment for a minor infection. Such treatment would have made no difference to our older brains, with their more established connections. But so soon after birth the connections of the eye were at a critical period for the establishment of eye-to-brain circuits.

Since neurons serving the bandaged eye were not working, their normal target became taken over by nerves from the normal, working eye, as we have seen already with the frog's eye and mouse whiskers. In this case, the neurons that were not working were treated by the brain as though they were not there at all: the target of these inactive, functionally nonexistent neurons was therefore readily invaded by the active brain cells. Sadly, the bandaging of the eye was misinterpreted by the brain as a clear indication that the boy would not be using that eye for the rest of his life.

Normally, this "use it or lose it" rule would be beneficial as it would mean that neuronal circuits were being established according to the working cells, which reflected in turn the environmental requirements in which the person had to live. In the expanding human brain, such sensitivity to local factors within brain circuitry is rampant. As our development continues after birth, the jostling, restless neurons in the brain are very reactive as they form circuits to reflect whatever is happening in the individual outside world. Inside the brain, right up to sixteen years of age, a bloody battle is being waged between our neurons. It is a battle for establishing connections. If a new neuron does not make contact with a target neuron, or is insufficiently stimulated, then it dies.

As we interact in this way with the environment, we become more adept at surviving in it, as more and more of the appropriate (that is, the most hardworking) neurons are connected to enable the most effective signaling. Even within a specific brain region, some brain circuits grow more than others. Such circuits are also the most electrically active (see Chapter 3), as well as being the most metabolically active, in that they are richer in chemicals for the manufacture of the energy-storing chemical adenosine triphosphate (ATP; see Chapter 1). In the brain, then, activity and growth go hand in hand: it is not only a question of "use it or lose it" but "use it as much as you can." (See Figure 10.)

Any small change in the normal lifestyle or environment will be reflected in a change in neuronal circuitry. For example, kittens were simply trained to lift up one paw

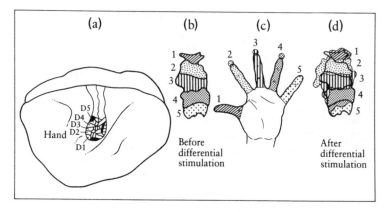

FIGURE 10

Incessant adaptation of the brain to experience. Each of the monkey's five digits (D1–D5) is represented in two adjacent areas in the part of the cortex devoted to processing touch: the "somatosensory cortex" (a). Diagrams (b) and (d) outline the neuronal allocations for each digit of an adult monkey corresponding to digits in (c), before (b), and after (d) training. During training, the monkey rotated a disc for one hour a day, with digits 2 and 3 and occasionally 4. Three months later, (d), the area representing the fingers that had received the extra stimulation from the rotating task in the brain, has increased markedly.

[Adapted from *Mind and Brain* by E. Kandel and R. D. Hawkins (New York: W. H. Freeman & Co., 1993)]

to show they could discriminate between patterns of horizontal versus vertical lines. Examination of their brain revealed an increase of about 30 percent more connections in the specific part of the cortex relating to sensations in that paw. Thus, it is connections that are important, and the degree of the stimulation from the environment will determine how the connections between neurons are formed, and thus determine your individual memories and so, as we shall see in the next chapter, make you into the person you are.

It is a popular idea that this selection of connections is taken from a wider pool of existing connections that are then "lost," rather like making a sculpture by removing or losing the extraneous marble or granite. Although many neuronal connections do undoubtedly die off in development, such a loss is more than offset by the runaway growth of the brain, as it forges the appropriate connections between neurons as a result of how much they are being used and consequently how active they are. Hence there is no generic brain that gets shaped into an individual one. Rather, the individual grows as the brain does, over some sixteen years in all.

At last then, we come to the mature brain that, at the age of sixteen, has finally increased in size by 5 percent over the preceding eleven years or so. Although the brain is particularly impressionable while developing, such adaptability does not cease but merely lessens somewhat in maturity. It is actually possible to manipulate the environment and still observe long-term changes in the mature brain. For example, adult rats were exposed to an "enriched environment" where they had an abundance of toys, wheels, ladders, and so forth with which to play. In contrast, other, similar rats were kept in an ordinary cage, where they received as much food and water as they wanted, but had no toys.

When the brains of these two groups of rats were examined, it was found that the number of connections in the brain had increased only in the animals in the enriched environment, not in those from the ordinary cages. It appears that sheer numbers of neurons are not as important as the connections between them in the brain, and these connections are highly changeable not just in development but also in adulthood. Specific experiences will enhance the connectivity in highly specific neuronal circuits.

We should be cautious about seemingly obvious social implications of this type of study. An enriched environment for a human would not simply be one with access to more material possessions or increased physical activity, such as repetitive dancing to a beat. Rather, the key factor is stimulation of the brain. In the study with rats, it was found that it was the activities that involved learning and memory, not mere physical activity, that resulted in the greatest changes in the brain. You do not have to be rich to stimulate your brain with "enriched environment." Human stimulation can be achieved informally outside of the schoolroom by lively conversations, meaningful relationships, crossword puzzles, and incessant reading, irrespective of whether such events occur in an inner city or on a beach in the Caribbean.

Thus, as we live out our lives, we fashion the connections between neurons that endow us with an individual, unique brain. Nonetheless, by the time we arrive at middle age we are fairly fixed as a personality, or we think we are: certainly, inside the middle-aged brain some processes are starting to slow down a little. Younger people will have faster reaction times. Although the middle-aged brain is still evolving and reacting to the environment, in terms of certain processes it is slowing down—for example, in the acquisition of new skills such as driving. Although younger people do not drive better, they are better at learning to drive: statistics from the British School of Motoring suggest that the average number of hours tuition (the number of hours a person pays for at the school to learn how to drive) roughly matches the student's age.

Our brain continues to slow down in certain ways but to adapt and change in others. Most of us nurture the hopes of living a long time, eventually reaching old age. It is well known that we are living longer. Indeed, the increased emphasis on brain disorders of the elderly is one of the most compelling reasons for studying the brain. In 1900, the life expectancy was forty-seven, and only 4 percent of the population was over sixty-five, whereas in 1990 more than 12 percent of the population was over sixty-five. Twenty percent of the population will be over sixty-five by the year 2020. More than any other generation, we have a greater chance of being in excellent health due to a good diet, better medical care, and an increasing interest in physical fitness.

However, it is at this final stage in life that the brain starts to diminish in its mass. There is a 20-percent loss in brain weight by age ninety, and even by age seventy there is a 5-percent loss in brain weight. On the other hand, as discussed in Chapter 1, we know that the remaining neurons can take over certain roles. Why does the brain age? There are various theories, such as the activation of ageing genes that run out of genetic information, or the genetic program suddenly becomes subject to random damage over time, or inactive or harmful proteins are suddenly produced. We still do not know the cause of the devastating diseases of old age—Alzheimer's disease and Parkinson's disease—where different parts of the brain are subject to massive neuronal loss. However, it is important to realize that these diseases are actually illnesses; they are not a natural consequence of old age.

In a recent study of Alzheimer patients, it was found that a certain region of the brain (the medial temporal lobe) was less than half the size of that of a non-Alzheimer patient of comparable age. Even more dramatic was the discovery that the rate of thinning of this brain region is far greater in Alzheimer's patients than in normal aging persons. Thus, Alzheimer's disease is a catastrophic event for the brain, with devastating consequences, but it is not the natural destiny of us all.

Nonetheless, brain cells do change in normal old age. It is believed by some that there is a reduction in the dendrites, the receiving area of neurons, although this idea is still hotly debated. If this is true, it might be thought that our processing abilities decline, but a recent study has shown that we can still process an incredible amount of information. We know that older rats can still form new connections in response to a rich environment, and although older people perform worse on some problem-solving tasks and process information a little slower, there is no evidence that learning ability decreases with age. In fact, vocabulary improves. Politicians, heads of business, heads of the church, and political leaders are very often in their sixties and seventies when presumably at the peak of their powers. It is perhaps telling that in ancient Rome you could be a judge only after reaching age sixty.

Even at the physical level there is no reason to assume that we are all destined to become debilitated. One lady, Hilda Crooks, climbed Mount Fuji at the age of ninety-one. Old age can be the ultimate expression of you as an individual. In the next chapter, we now turn to see how that individuality can be expressed in terms of the physical brain.

CHAPTER 5

....

WITH MIND IN MIND

Where is the root of individuality? By looking at a single human brain it is educated guesswork at best to determine whether the person was male or female. It would, however, be completely impossible to tell whether this particular man or woman had been kind or possessed a sense of humor. As we saw in Chapter 1, all brains comply with the same basic ground plan: there are nerves carrying in information about the senses, and other nerves coming out that contract the muscles and are responsible for movement. We have also seen that the brain is made up of neurons, and that the circuitry in which these neurons operate is in part genetic but to a very great extent—at least in relatively complex brains—also influenced by the environment. How might such circuitry be translated into an individual? We address this issue in this chapter.

Identical twins are clones of each other. They are two people with identical genes because the single fertilized egg split into two. But are they identical people? Certainly, imaging with nuclear magnetic resonance (NMR) scans (see Chapter 1) of the brains of identical twins show a greater similarity at the gross structural level. If identical twins are questioned about their preferences, attitudes, and experiences there are, perhaps not surprisingly, often considerable similarities. However, a coincidence in tastes and ideas might not be that remarkable in any siblings reared in the same environment.

Identical twins will also show signs of distinct perceptions and thoughts that make it clear they are individuals with their own private consciousness, even though their genetic makeup is the same. If individuality is not accountable by genes, it must, at least in part, be due to some other factor in the brain that is not shared even by descendants of the same egg.

We have already seen in the previous chapter how experience is a key factor in shaping the microcircuitry of the brain. Eating something that you associate with an unpleasant event could well make you dislike that particular type of food. Even more simply, only those exposed to the music of Mozart, for example, will ever have the chance to say that they have a preference for Mozart. Experiences we have never had can play no part in framing our personality: if someone inherited a potential for learning many languages, that linguistic ability would not be realized if the person was never exposed to different languages.

The process of evolving a unique brain is perhaps most dramatic up to and including the teenage years, but even then the brain is not caught in freeze frame. Our character continues to adapt as we respond to, and recoil from, the incessant experiences thrown in our path. For experiences to have any lasting significance in this way, they need to be remembered. The essence of the individual thus lies in no small part with what he or she can remember. Perhaps we could start with memory as a way of approaching the secret of the physical basis of individuality.

In English at least, *memory* can serve as an umbrella term for a diverse range of processes that may well be quite distinct. Compare the memory processes of an octopus and a human. The octopus has one of the largest brains of all invertebrates, roughly equal in size to the brain of a fish, and composed of some 170 million nerve cells. Although this number seems large, it is trivial in comparison with the human neuronal count of some 100 billion. Nonetheless, the octopus has proved popular in learning and memory experiments, because it has highly developed eyes and a sophisticated system of touch via its many tentacles. In experiments, an octopus can clearly tell the difference between certain colors and can attach different meanings to each. For example, it will readily grasp at a colored ball it has previously learned is associated with delivery of a prawn, but will not react to a ball of a different color that has not been paired with anything either rewarding or aversive.

This type of memory, a simple association between a colored ball and a prawn, may seem a far cry from the memory of a particular hot summer day by the sea, or how to ride a bicycle, or remembering the French for "window." There are many distinct types of brain processes that fall under the general term *memory*. The most basic and familiar distinction is between short-term and long-term memory. Short-term memory operates when we try to remember a series of numbers. Everything is fine if there are no distractions, because the strategy is usually to repeat the sequence in our mind over and over again. This process is surprisingly modest: we can only remember an average of seven digits.

One of the most obvious questions to ask about short-term memory is how it relates to long-term memory. This less contrived type of memory process occurs without any need for repetition or rehearsal. Do short- and long-term memory operate in parallel, in a completely independent way? It is well known that patients who remember nothing about what has happened to them beyond the immediate present, and who thereby exhibit an almost global amnesia, nonetheless have a short-term memory ability indistinguishable from nonamnesiacs. Clearly then, the two processes can be separated, but could someone have a normal long-term memory even when short-term memory ability is destroyed?

Impairments in short-term memory are difficult to study. Long-term memory is not a one-step process but, just as we saw for other brain functions in Chapter 2, it can be divided into many different aspects. For each of these different aspects there appears to be a respective form of short-term memory. For example, young children who have a poor short-term memory for nonsense words also have a poor long-term memory for unfamiliar names of toys. Short-term and long-term memory appear to work not independently in parallel but in series. First, short-term memory comes into operation: it is a transient, highly unstable and vulnerable process where attention and rehearsal are needed in order to lead into the more permanent and dormant long-term memory. Successful rehearsal in short-term memory will eventually lead to that special phone number being retained without constant attention to it.

We all know that short-term memory is improved if numbers, for example, have significance, such as a telephone number or a security number to a building or a safe. In any case, if an item survives in your memory for more than about thirty minutes, it is probably not going to be forgotten, at least for a matter of days. Patients recovering from concussion or electric shock treatment (a radical therapy for severe depression) characteristically cannot remember what happened an hour or so before the event, whereas their long-term memory remains operational. In these cases there is presumably a disruption of only the first step in the memory process, the short-term memory stage. This early rupture in the normal course of events subsequently obliterates any chance of that hour of life being recorded more permanently in the mind of the individual.

Short-term memory operates to serve long-term memory. But what do we mean by long-term memory? It turns out that, once more, this other basic category for the umbrella idea of memory can itself be further broken down into two distinct phenomena. There is much that we learn and remember as we go through life: how to drive a car, the French for "thank you," and what we did when Aunt Flo last came to visit. All these are examples of different types of memory at work. However, the odd item in these three examples would be how to drive a car. The memory for a fact, such as the French for "thank you," or an event, such as the recent visit of Aunt Flo, requires that we should be making an explicit conscious effort. In contrast, driving a car, like many skills and habits, is almost performed on automatic pilot. This type of memory is therefore referred to as *implicit,* because we do not need to actively and consciously remember how to do something: we just get in a car and drive. When you approach a red light your foot is "automatically" on the brake. In contrast to this process, memory for events and facts can be regarded as *explicit* memory.

One of the most famous and intensively investigated cases of complete loss of explicit memory is that of H.M., a young man who had severe epilepsy, the condition in which the patient is stricken with a seizure accompanied by loss of consciousness. In H.M.'s case, these epileptic seizures became so frequent that it was impossible for him to live a normal life.

In 1953, at the age of twenty-seven, H.M. had part of his brain removed to control the epileptic seizures. Despite its success in combatting epilepsy, this operation has never been performed since then, because of the terrible consequence: after surgery, H.M. could remember only events before his operation—up to about two years beforehand. Since the surgery he has remained constantly trapped in the present.

It is very hard to imagine H.M.'s state of mind. He fails

to recognize friends or neighbors that he has gotten to know after the operation. Although he can give the date of his birth, he cannot give his correct age, always estimating that he is younger than he actually is. During the night he might ask the nurse where he is and why he is there. He cannot reconstruct the events of the previous day. He explains, "Every day is alone by itself, whatever enjoyment I have had, whatever sorrow I have had." For H.M., there are no yesterdays.

As a result of this condition, H.M. has only been able to carry out simple acts in the here and now. Therefore, he was given monotonous jobs such as mounting cigarette lighters on cardboard displays. He could not give a description of the place in which he worked, the nature of his job, or the route along which he was driven every day.

H.M. can still remember strings of up to seven digits, thus demonstrating that short-term memory is a separate process from the subsequent stage of long-term memory. Moreover, although H.M. appears to have lost his ability to remember in the long term, his brain has retained a different type of memory. H.M. can actually perform quite well at certain motor skills like tracing a star. However, this task is not as easy as it sounds since the outline has to be traced while looking in a mirror: it is a demanding exercise in sensory motor coordination that improves with practice, like driving or riding a bicycle. Every day, H.M. did indeed improve, showing that this other type of memory, implicit memory, was not processed in the same part of the brain as memories for events. Interestingly enough, H.M. was not conscious of remembering the *event* of learning to draw the star (an example of explicit memory), although his brain was quite happily getting better at doing so—implicit memory.

Particularly relevant to our present discussion is that although H.M. cannot remember events occurring after, and two years prior to, his surgery, past memories from long ago are still intact, trapped in the brain like a fly in amber.

These memories are obviously not dependent on the brain area that has been removed. It must be the case that no one brain region can assume the entire responsibility for the whole memory process of facts and events. Rather, memories must be somehow processed through one region but consolidated elsewhere. In H.M.'s case, the damage must have intervened at the stage where a new memory is first processed. Hence, all the memories that had already been consolidated were safe. Just as we saw in Chapter 2 in our consideration of the senses and the control of movement, different brain regions are responsible for different aspects of a function.

The area that H.M. had removed was the middle part of his temporal lobe, which lies on either side of the brain, as its name suggests, by the temples, just above the ears. This area also includes a region underneath the cortex called the *hippocampus,* which is Greek for "seahorse," because some people think this structure looks like a seahorse. It is, to my mind, actually easiest to visualize the hippocampus as it nestles in the brain below the cortex as a structure shaped more like rams' horns, curling around the inner mass of the brain. A considerable amount of clinical and experimental evidence has shown, subsequent to the case of H.M., that damage to this brain region results in an impairment in the laying down of memories.

Even for this more specific aspect of memory, its initial consolidation, there is another area that appears to be important: the medial thalamus, which is vital for the relaying of incoming sensory information onto the cortex (see Chapter 2). Just as the processing of hearing and vision each rely on a different part of the thalamus, so there is a specific area of the thalamus contributing to memory.

We know that the medial thalamus contributes to memory because of one or two unfortunate and bizarre accidents in which people have ended up with either fencing foils or snooker cues up one nostril, thereby destroying the medial thalamus. In such cases, the victims of these accidents have displayed amnesia for events. Unlike the examples of amnesia we have looked at so far, the problem has often been only temporary, however. Despite the fact that the amnesia can be temporary, there is a permanent inability for memory of events that occurred while the amnesia lasted, presumably while the medial thalamus was malfunctioning. Hence, as for the hippocampus, the medial thalamus can be viewed as important in the consolidation of memories.

Source amnesia is a loss of memory for when and where an event occurred. If there is no space or time reference, events cannot be differentiated, and there is no personal involvement of the individual with what has happened. Because events are unique and personal, whereas facts are generic and free of time and space frames of reference, it follows that source amnesia will primarily affect memory for events rather than for facts. Whereas memory for both facts and events appear to rely on the integrity of the hippocampus and the medial temporal lobe, only memory for events seems affected by damage to this third area, the prefrontal cortex, which we encountered in Chapter 1.

Interestingly enough, damage to the medial thalamus, which has connections with the prefrontal cortex, can also result in special types of errors in the time-space allocation of memories. Memories can come forward inappropriately, out of context, when they are irrelevant to the speech and ideas of the present moment. The prefrontal cortex is presumably having some influence not just in the way events are remembered, as occurring at a certain time and place, but also in how they are associated with related events at presumably a similar time or place.

Facts, as in semantic memory, need differ only from the events of episodic memory in that they are removed from a specific moment and place. Once the pink elephant is displaced from the jungle hideaway in which you saw him one night in the last summer vacation, he becomes reduced to the generic thought that elephants can be pink. Damage to the area where facts have been personalized into events by time and space referencing would not actually destroy memory itself but rather would uncouple facts from the contexts in which they occurred. Specific events would be reduced to mere generic facts in that they would have no special or unique features in time and space.

If the prefrontal cortex is needed for this type of time-space allocation to the memory of events, and if, as we saw in Chapter 1, the prefrontal cortex has shown an extraordinary differential growth during evolution, it follows that this type of memory for events would be particularly pronounced in humans, with our disproportionately large prefrontal cortex, and of far less prominence in other animals. For other animals, perhaps memory of an event is more generic, less anchored by unique time and place coordinates. A cat may not remember a specific spring day when it caught a mouse in the back garden just after drinking a saucer of milk and before climbing a tree, although it may well have a vaguer and more general recall of catching mice. Interestingly, there is a specific, contrived situation where our human memories also seem to be more like this generic type of memory.

These pioneering studies were performed in Canada in the mid-1900s by Wilder Penfield, a surgeon. Penfield worked with five hundred patients who were undergoing neurosurgery. It is often a ghoulish surprise to many that there are no sensors for pain within the brain itself; hence it is possible for the brain to be exposed in conscious patients without them feeling any pain. With the patients' consent, Penfield used the operations, which had to be performed in any case, to investigate the storage of memory in the brain. Since the surface of the brain was exposed and the patients were fully conscious, he was able to stimulate different parts of the cortex electrically while documenting the reports of the patients as to what they were experiencing.

Most of the time, perhaps not surprisingly, the patients did not report any new experience. Sometimes, however, a rather interesting phenomenon occurred: the patients claimed they could remember very vivid scenes. They often said that these memories were like a dream; they were more generalized experiences that did not have particular time and space points of reference. Perhaps in this highly artificial situation, the electrical stimulation was locally kick-starting the medial temporal lobe, without recruiting other requisite but more remote regions. Of these remote brain regions, the prefrontal cortex in particular would normally be operative during memory of an event. We have seen in Chapter 1, and just now, that without the prefrontal cortex our memories still exist but are vaguer and less specific, perhaps resembling the dreamlike memories of Penfield's patients, or even normal dreams. If a reduction in the role of the prefrontal cortex, for whatever reason, did indeed induce a more dreamlike state of mind, it would follow that animals with a less pronounced prefrontal cortex do not have the precise memories that we have. Instead, their memories would be disembodied facts that lack a time-space context: "episodic" memory for an event would have almost become "semantic" memory for a fact.

As we saw in Chapter 1, the prefrontal cortex appears to be important in working memory, where incoming information and ongoing behavior are influenced by certain internalized and individual ideas, perceptions, or rules, the inner resources accrued over a lifetime that constitute an idiosyncratic mind. These inner resources would provide some sort of counterweight to the bombardment of the brain by a torrent of implosive sensory information. Damage to the prefrontal cortex has often been compared with schizophrenia and, conversely, schizophrenia has in part been attributed to a malfunctioning of the prefrontal cortex (see Chapter 1). A common and conspicuous feature of schizophrenia is excessive attention to the outside world, which often appears overly bright and buzzing, without the sobering perspective and experience-based interpretation of inner resources. Perhaps dreamers, schizophrenics, and nonhumans share a similar type of consciousness, characterized by little memory for previous events, and dominated by generic facts and the immediacy of the here and now. If so, such a profile of awareness might have contributed to the character change of Phineas Gage (see Chapter 1) following the severe damage to his prefrontal cortex.

So far we have seen that for explicit memory of both events and facts, clinical cases (for example, H.M.) suggest that the hippocampus and medial thalamus play a role in laying down memories for about two years; these long-term memories are somehow "stored" in the temporal lobe, as revealed by Penfield's studies. Meanwhile, the prefrontal cortex, with which the hippocampus and medial thalamus both have connections, coordinates facts with an appropriate time and space context to ensure that an event is remembered as a unique happening.

How might a fact or an event be stored in the brain? We know that even though memories of past events might survive damage to the thalamus and hippocampus, they are far from indestructible. It is helpful to compare H.M.'s memory loss, where there was removal of the medial temporal lobe, with another type of memory loss from another group of patients. These patients have memory problems due to chronic alcoholism. Among the many risks of taking alcohol in great abundance is a disease associated with a dietary deficiency of thiamine: Korsakoff's syndrome. Patients with this disease not only have the same type of memory impairment as H.M.—namely amnesia for everything that happened since his surgery (anterograde amnesia)—but also loss of memory for everything that happened before being taken into the hospital, and even before the onset of the illness (retrograde amnesia).

The distinction between anterograde and retrograde amnesia was demonstrated in a study carried out in the 1970s. Korsakoff patients proved worse than H.M. at recognizing the faces of celebrities who had been famous in the 1930s and 1940s. The problem in learning about memory from Korsakoff patients is that it is hard to isolate the deficits from other types of thinking processes. With alcoholics, the brain damage is so widespread that there are many conditions affected other than memory. Korsakoff patients, unlike H.M., would have extensive damage to a variety of other brain regions, including large areas of the cortex.

Is there a particular brain region where a memory is finally laid down? Psychologist Karl Lashley tried to answer this question in the 1940s. Lashley trained rats on a memory task in mazes, and then removed different portions of cortex to see if he could identify where the memory engram might be stored. To his surprise and consternation, removal of different parts of the cortex did not result in a precise matching between one specific area and the retention of a specific memory. Rather, the more cortex that was removed, irrespective of specificity of region, the worse the rats became at the memory task. Perhaps not surprisingly, the entire cortex plays an important role in the storage of memory.

In line with Lashley's evidence from rats, the clinical cases reported by Penfield would also suggest that memory is not stored simply; it is not laid down directly in the brain. Rather, as seen in Penfield's studies, a cachet of memories would be more like a nebulous series of dreams. One immediate problem was that the memories themselves were not like highly specific recordings on a video and were a far cry from the memories on a computer. Another problem was that if the same area was stimulated by Penfield on different occasions, different memories were elicited. Conversely, the same memories could be generated from stimulating different areas. No one has yet shown definitively how these phenomena can be explained in terms of brain functioning. One possibility, however, is that each time Penfield stimulated the same site, he was activating a different circuitry of neurons, where each circuit might participate in a particular memory. Similarly, when stimulating in another locus, Penfield may have sometimes been activating a circuit he had activated before, but simply from a different triggering point—once the same circuit was activated, from whatever triggering point, the memory would be the same.

An interpretation of Penfield's findings is that memory is somehow associated with overlapping circuits of neurons. One neuron could be a member of a number of different circuits; it would be the specific combination in each case that distinguished one circuit from another. Each circuit would contribute to the phenomenon of a memory, so that no single brain cell or exclusively committed group of cells is wholly responsible; instead, the memory would be distributed. The biochemist Stephen Rose reached this conclusion when he trained chicks to go against their natural inclination and to avoid pecking at a bead.

In brief, Rose found that different parts of the chick brain were processing and remembering different features of the bead, such as its size as opposed to its color. Just as we saw for the visual process itself in Chapter 3, memory for the sight of an object was also laid down in parallel. There is no single region for a memory but rather it is distributed over many regions. According to the modality of what is remembered, and the associations it triggers for a certain context, different levels of circuitry will be recruited over the entire cortex. It is easy to see how Lashley could have been under the impression that virtually all the cortex was somehow working together in the memory process.

How do the memories actually become consolidated in the cortex in the first place? We have seen that all types of memory first enter the highly transient and dissociable phase of short-term memory, but short-term memory only lasts at most for half an hour. In contrast is the striking case of H.M., where, although he had perfect recall of all that had happened early in his life, he could not remember anything from the period of two years preceding his operation. For the hippocampus and medial thalamus to consolidate memories, it is not just a matter of a few minutes but of a substantial period of time.

No one really knows exactly how the hippocampus and medial thalamus might be working over a period of years, in conjunction with the cortex, to lay down memories that will eventually no longer depend on the integrity of these subcortical structures. One attractive idea draws on a memory being composed of otherwise arbitrary elements, brought together for the first time in the event or the fact to be remembered. The role of the hippocampus and medial thalamus would be to ensure that these disparate, previ-

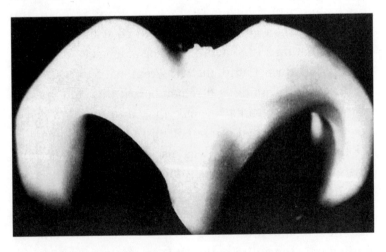

FIGURE II

The hippocampus dissected out from a rat brain.
[Photo courtesy of Dr. Nick Rawlins, Oxford]

ously unassociated elements are now associated and thus somehow bound into a cohesive memory. Just as we saw in the simple case of the color versus shape of the beads in Rose's experiment, different parts of the cortex would be involved. Some mechanism would therefore be needed to recruit these different and remote neuronal populations into a working network.

It is possible to imagine that initially the cohesiveness of the working cortical network that represents the memory depends on an ongoing dialogue with the hippocampus and medial thalamus. However, as the network becomes established, seemingly over a period of several years, gradually the subcortical structures become less important, such that eventually, as we saw with H.M., an established memory can remain intact, freed up from, and entirely independent of, the hippocampus. One metaphor might be that of scaffolding: while a building is being established, the removal of the scaffolding would lead to the collapse of the edifice; however, once the building is completed, the scaffolding is redundant.

If explicit memory for events and facts depends on an initial dialogue between the cortex and certain subcortical structures, perhaps this same arrangement could also apply to the laying down of skills and habits: implicit memory. Certain habits, such as remembering sequences or making a certain type of movement in an appropriate context without needing to think about it, can be performed adequately in amnesiac patients with medial temporal lobe damage. However, patients suffering from disorders of the basal ganglia such as Parkinson's disease and Huntington's chorea (see Chapter 2) have seemingly no problem explicitly remembering facts and events. Instead, their problem is that they are no longer able to perform the habit of an appropriate sequence of movement, or of recognizing the next item in a sequence that had been shown to them over and over again and normally would have been implicitly remembered.

An everyday example of a habit is the ability to generate the right type of movement at the right time. Patients with Huntington's chorea no longer generate a movement in an appropriate context—for example, the flinging of a limb that can characterize that disorder might be appropriate on the baseball pitch, but not in the shopping mall. On the other hand, Parkinsonian patients can no longer sequence a movement: the more complex the sequence—for example, standing up, or turning around—the greater the impairment. In both of these very different disorders of the basal ganglia there is a lapse in the implicit memory system, a fault in different aspects (respectively, context and sequence) of the habit of generating movements.

The basal ganglia are not the only brain regions to be involved in implicit memory. Some memory tasks involve conditioning, rather like we saw for the octopus at the beginning of this chapter: presentation of an erstwhile neutral stimulus, such as a ball, evoked a response once it had been associated with a meaningful stimulus, such as a prawn. Certain types of conditioning involving an immediate movement of the muscles are now thought to be controlled by the cerebellum, the little brain on the back of the head (see Chapters 1 and 2). For example, it is possible in both rabbits and humans to condition the eye to blink to an erstwhile neutral stimulus, such as the sound of a bell, when it is associated with a natural trigger for the eye blink, such as a puff of air.

We can see that for habits and skills, different brain structures are involved compared to those used in explicit memory of facts and events. A critical difference lies not just in the identity of these structures but also in their relation to the cortex. Whereas the medial thalamus and hippocampus have strong reciprocal connections with the cortex, the connections with the basal ganglia and cerebellum are not so robust or dominant. The striatum, which is the pivotal part of the basal ganglia in both Huntington's chorea and Parkinson's disease, receives an input from the cortex, but does not send one directly back. Similarly, the cerebellum, while indirectly linked to the cortex, does not have any direct connections. Hence it is tempting to imagine that these brain regions, unlike those involved in explicit memory, are left in a sense to freewheel more autonomously. This scenario might be expected of activities such as implicit memory that are performed without attention or conscious effort: such activities would not need constant referral to the cortex, which is known to play a key role in conscious attention. As we saw in Chapter 2, once a movement can become automated, either by internalized triggers in the basal ganglia or from sensory inputs fed through the cerebellum, the cortex is free for other functions, such as explicit memory, the remembering of facts and events.

We have seen that memory can be subdivided into different processes and that each process will be served by different combinations of brain regions. But common to all these memory processes is perhaps the most mysterious issue of all: We know that some people can remember what happened to them ninety years ago, but by then every molecule in their body will have been turned over many times. If long-term changes mediating memories are occurring continuously in the brain, how are they sustained? Irrespective of brain region, how do neurons register more or less permanent change as a result of experience?

We have been considering memory using top-down strategies. In order to answer this latest question, we have to travel bottom-up. Imagine a synapse that was participating in a memory process of any kind. Let us think, for simplicity's sake, of a memory in its simplest form as an association between two previously unassociated elements. Again, purely for simplicity, let us think of each of these elements as represented by two single cells.

During a memory, the two previously unassociated

neurons would be simultaneously active, and that coincidental activity would eventually have some long-lasting result far outliving the periods for which each cell was active in the first place. The easiest scenario to imagine is that explained in the 1940s by the visionary psychologist Donald Hebb. He proposed that when an incoming cell, X, was particularly active, and excited a target cell, Y, then the synapse between X and Y would become strengthened. By strengthening, Hebb meant that this synapse would be more effective in chemical signaling than the other, more dormant inputs making contact with Y. This idea is a version of what we have already seen in the previous chapter during development, when the hardest working neuron (in this case, X) ends up with the most effective connections.

The second, more recent proposal for an alternative way in which to strengthen a connection is for the strengthened contact not to involve the target cell Y directly, but to involve the use of a third cell, Z. This third cell would impinge on X *before* it signaled to Y. Hence this strengthening would be presynaptic, not postsynaptic as in Hebb's scheme. If Z and X were coincidentally active such that Z modulated (see Chapter 3) the activity of X, more transmitters would be released onto the final target Y. Only when X and Z were active at the same time would X consequently release more transmitter onto Y. (See Figure 12.)

This scenario has been most effectively demonstrated in the sea slug, Aplysia, which has the advantage of a far simpler nervous system, such that single neurons are even identified by name. In the simpler nervous system of Aplysia, there is no problem in uniting top-down with bottom-up: the activity in the neuronal circuits translates directly into demonstrable behavior. Here is one example: A nerve Z (comparable to Z above) that responds to a naturally aversive stimulus in the tail impinges on a sensory nerve (X) that responds to a benign stimulus. This sensory

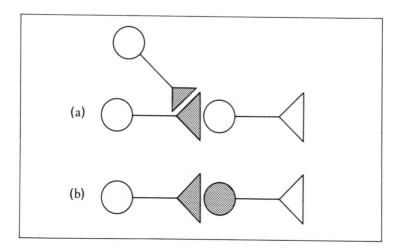

FIGURE 12

Possible bases of adaptation of neurons to experience, reflected in the activity of incoming cells. In Aplysia (a), the coincident activity of two cells where one intercepts the other, more transmitters are released onto the target cell. In the mammalian brain (b), a cell that has already been activated will be able to respond more readily to further stimulation, as shown in the shaded area.

[Drawn by Dr. O. Paulsen,
MRC Anatomical Neuropharmacology Unit, Oxford]

nerve then links up directly with the motor nerve *(Y)* with which Aplysia retracts its gill.

Aplysia can be conditioned to retract its gill to an otherwise neutral stimulus on the sensory nerve, rather like we can be conditioned to blink our eyes to the neutral stimulus of a bell ringing. When Z and X are coincidentally active (that is, when the benign and aversive stimuli occur simultaneously), Z induces in nerve X a cascade of chemical reactions that leads to the closure of potassium channels (see Chapter 3). When the efflux of this positively charged ion is prevented, the voltage across the cell membrane becomes more positive: this is precisely the voltage requirement needed for the opening of special channels for calcium to enter the cell. When more calcium consequently enters the cell, more transmitter is released (see Chapter 3). More transmitter released by the sensory nerve X onto the motor nerve Y means that the motor nerve will work harder, and the resultant behavior, withdrawal of the gill, will be stronger. Nerve X can remain in this potentiated state even when Z ceases to be active. The behavior will have been conditioned.

Similarly, in the mammalian brain, it is plausible that at any of the many synapses in the many brain regions involved in memory, there will be a strengthening of certain hardworking synapses. A pivotal mechanism by which this scenario is thought to be achieved is called long-term potentiation (LTP). LTP works by exploiting the fussy nature of a certain type of target receptor (NMDA; that is, N-methyl-D-aspartate) for a certain type of transmitter (glutamate). Unlike the more normal scenario in Chapter 3, this receptor will only trigger ion channels to open when two conditions are fulfilled. First, as is normally the case, the incoming cell must also be active so that the transmitter in question—in this case, glutamate—can be released to dock into its receptor. Second is the unusual requirement that the cell must already have a more positive voltage than usual. Only when these two requirements are met does the fussy receptor allow a large amount of calcium to flood into the target cell.

These two requirements could be achieved only if there is coincident activity in either of two ways. One way would be for two incoming cells to be active simultaneously, so that each would meet one of the two requirements—one incoming cell would release the glutamate while the other caused a decrease in voltage by releasing another transmitter. The second way to fulfill both requirements would be with just the cell that released glutamate. Initially the fussy channel would not open, since, although glutamate was released, the voltage of the cell would be normal. The glutamate would just work, in the normal way, on a less fussy type of glutamate receptor. If the release of this glutamate was *sustained,* then the effects of activating the less fussy receptor would be to decrease the voltage of the target cell, thereby fulfilling the second requirement. The fussy glutamate receptor could then open the channel for calcium ions to flood in. Hence, sustained activity, as well as coincident activity of incoming cells, could in either case trigger a change in the long-term response of a target neuron.

This type of sustained or coincident activity of incoming neurons might occur in a memory situation. The ensuing large influx of calcium again will trigger a chemical cascade within the target cell such that another chemical is released that ricochets across the synapse, enters the incoming cell, and acts to make it release even more transmitters. The target cell is in turn even more active and the synapse is said to be strengthened. When the incoming cell of the strengthened synapse is stimulated again, only modestly, the response that now ensues will be greater, a little akin to the enhanced gill withdrawal of Aplysia. This is known as potentiation.

This type of phenomenon might account for short-term memory. However, we know that short-term memory is just that—lasting less than an hour. In order to account for our seemingly permanent memories, more permanent changes must be taking place at the cellular level. LTP in the mammalian brain, as for the potentiation in Aplysia, would be a necessary but not sufficient factor. If the enhanced release of transmitter were sustained, as it might well be in the laying down of a memory, then the transmitter would not only have to be passing on the message to the target cell on the other side of the synapse for a more vigorous or potentiated response in the short term. In addition, the long-lasting result of this enhanced activity would actually have to be a change in what was happening inside the target cell.

Clearly, permanent changes cannot rely on existing chemicals simply being released in greater quantities. Even if certain enzymes become spontaneously active, which they do, thereby increasing the efficiency of the synapse, such molecules only have a life span ranging from minutes to weeks. Although much of what happens within the cell during memory is still a mystery, certain facts are emerging. For both Aplysia and the LTP in mammalian brains, we have seen that the underlying common event is the entry of calcium into the neuron.

This entry can act as a trigger, in as little as thirty minutes, for activating certain genes by using proteins that in themselves are short-lived. Nonetheless, the products of such genes are then able to activate other genes, which, by the diverse ways in which they are expressed, can modify a neuron for a very long period. The effects of activating genes within the neuron might be to increase the efficiency of the transmitter, increase the number of receptors, or even increase the efficiency with which a receptor opens an ion channel. However, the alternative way in which a neuron might be changed by gene expression is even more radical.

We learned in the previous chapter that the effects of experience are to modify not so much the numbers of neurons themselves but rather the connections between them. As a broad generalization, we saw that the more experience, the more connections. It is now known that within an hour of training on a particular task, certain important proteins are pressed into service. Two good examples of these proteins are the sticky badges, the cell adhesion molecules that we looked at in the previous chapter, and another aptly named growth-associated protein, GAP-43. Cell adhesion molecules appear to be important for neuron recognition and for the stabilization of neuronal contacts. As cell adhesion molecules are made in the brain, certain sugars are incorporated. We know that cell adhesion molecules are important in memory because if sugar incorporation is prevented by administering an appropriate drug, then amnesia results.

GAP-43 is an example of another protein that may play a role in memory—as its name suggests, it is implicated in the growth of neurons. Growth cones (see Chapter 4) contain GAP-43, and its synthesis is known to occur at a high rate when neurons are extending their axons. GAP-43 is apparently activated during LTP. Hence, it is tempting to speculate that the entry of calcium during the strengthening of a contact during a memory task will lead to enhanced growth of neuronal contacts, perhaps via GAP-43, and stabilization of those contacts, perhaps by means of cell adhesion molecules.

In this way there will be new synaptic contacts, which we saw in Chapter 4 were, during development, the way the brain most conspicuously reflected changes in the environment. It would not be surprising, as we go through life, for the process of adapting to experience, namely memory, to be an echo in our brain of the developmental process.

How might increased connections between neurons underpin the memory process? This is a difficult question to answer as it means bridging the gap, in the mammalian brain, between the cellular bottom-up level we have been discussing and the functional top-down approach addressed earlier in this chapter. We need to know how to relate the world of microscopic events in a multitude of neurons to the macrophenomenological world of memory. Although in Aplysia it is relatively straightforward to translate the activity of a certain neuronal circuit into a mechanical behavior such as retracting the gill, it is impossible in the human brain to pin down the behavior of having a certain memory to a specific neuronal circuit. Nonetheless, some features of the memory process do provide indications that connectivity between neurons, albeit sophisticated and currently unidentified, is important.

It is a well-known trick for improving memory to associate the item to be remembered with something that would itself trigger many associations. For example, associating a number ("3") with something that can be readily visualized ("three blind mice"), and which is very familiar (an old nursery rhyme), will improve the subsequent recall of the number. An alternative strategy is to imagine items of, say, a shopping list, distributed in different parts of a room, such that a bar of chocolate might be nailed to the door, the butter may be placed under the table, with the milk on the table and the tea in the sink. An alternative way of improving memory is to either place yourself, or imagine yourself, in the same context in which the remembered event originally occurred. You might imagine you were on the beach during summer vacation in order to recall the name of the lifeguard with whom you struck up a conversation. A more sophisticated version of this idea is to imagine other items belonging to the context in which the respective remembering took place (suntan lotion, towel, sunglasses). In all these cases we would be either creating a maximal number of associations during the act of consolidating a memory or exploiting such associations during recall.

It is well known that most people cannot remember events that occurred before they were about three years old. This phenomenon cannot be accounted for by simple length of time, since we are able subsequently to remember events for some ninety years. Moreover, young children are able to remember habits and skills from an early age—it is only explicit memory that is the problem. On the other hand, babies as young as five months are able, arguably, to show explicit memory by looking at a new item more than one they have previously seen, when the two items are presented together. Children under a year old may copy games they saw someone else playing, even only once, on a previous day.

It seems then that some simple form of explicit memory is available to young children, which in turn would mean that their hippocampus and medial thalamus must be operational. With regard to maturity, more in doubt is the cortex. If neurons in the cortex were unable to form many associations, then the explicit memory of children would not be, as indeed it is not, very robust. After the age of three the ability to associate items with a richer repertoire garnered from experience, aided in turn by an increased number of neuronal connections in the cortex, would make memory, as we know it, possible.

Although these strategies and examples might vary, the basic theme is the same: to capitalize on associations with the remembered item. At the neuronal level, these associations are certainly not a crude one-to-one matching of single cells. However, within the vast interplay of neuronal circuits of varying complexity, the basic unit of change will boil down to the modifications to connectivity we have been discussing. We know that long-term memory is accompanied by an increase in the number of presynaptic terminals, and we know that memory involves establishing new associations. We cannot establish as yet a causal relation between the physical and the phenomenological in the human brain; however, for the moment, it is sufficient to be aware of the correlation between these two levels of operation. Memory is multifaceted and multistaged. It is more than a mere function of the brain, as it encapsulates individuals' inner resources for interpreting, in an exquisitely unique fashion, the world around them. As such, memory is a good place to end our brief glimpse of the brain, for it is a cornerstone of the mind.

CONCLUSION

....

LOOKING FORWARD

In the preceding chapters we have had the chance to appreciate some of the awesome questions confronting brain researchers. In Chapters 1 and 2, we saw that the brain did not work as a collection of mini-brains but that somehow multiple brain regions contributed to different functions (parallel processing). No one has any idea, however, how disparate regions in the brain manage to give rise to a whole, a function such as movement or vision, that is more than the sum of the parts.

In Chapter 3, we surveyed how a brain is built. Although the neuronal nuts and bolts are now very familiar to most neuroscientists, their mode of operations is still continuing to surprise. In the 1970s a rather dogmatic certainty had crept into brain research that all functions in the brain were derived from the basic processes of excitation (increasing the number of action potentials in any one neuron) and inhibition (decreasing the number of action potentials), so that the increasingly large number of transmitter chemicals seemed redundant. Only now are we truly appreciating the complexity of actions of these chemicals. The concept of neuromodulation, of biasing the responses of neurons, is still being explored in relation to a diverse range of bioactive substances. As we saw in Chapter 3, the

147

fountainlike arrangement in the brain stem of amines and of acetylcholine are well placed to fulfil such functions. The challenge is to discover how the modulatory actions of these fountains, so often the target for mood-modifying drugs, can be related to the global functioning of the brain.

In Chapter 4 we saw how the synapses featured in the previous chapter were built into ever more complex circuits that evolve in childhood to give rise to unique yet impressionable individuals. On the one hand, there are very specific questions to be resolved, such as how a neuron knows when to alight from its glial monorail to the correct region of brain, and how it recognizes similar neurons with which it will team up into a particular circuitry. On the other hand, there are more general puzzles that remain complete enigmas. At what stage does the individuality creep into the developing brain? How do neuronal circuits give rise not just to an individual brain but to an individual consciousness? Of what might a fetus be conscious? Although I attempted to suggest one possible scenario, the idea of fetal consciousness being at the lower end of a continuum of consciousness is far from proven.

The riddle of a physical basis for consciousness and for mind was even more pressing when, in Chapter 5, we explored memory. Any study of memory will throw up two very large issues in neuroscience. The first issue is how we are unable to reconcile the top-down approach with the bottom-up approach. In sea slugs, it is possible to translate the operations of biochemical machinery into a remembered behavior, such as withdrawing a gill. In more sophisticated mammalian brains, however, we cannot show that a certain number of cellular mechanisms are not just necessary but sufficient for memory. This is because memory appears to be the emergent property of a number of brain regions working in parallel. Hence, top-down organization is as relevant as bottom-up mechanisms. Until the two can be woven into a cohesive description, attempts to understand that rich tapestry of human memory will inevitably flounder.

The second big issue posed by a consideration of memory is perhaps the most challenging of all: the relation of brain to mind. Memory is clearly a product of the physical brain (witness the story of H.M.), but compared to more explicit sensory or motor functions, it would be readily regarded as an aspect of the mind. One way of regarding the mind might be to equate it with the inner resources discussed in Chapters 1 and 5. We saw that this stockpile of memories, prejudices, and experiences would serve as a counterweight to the flood of everyday sensory experience. We also saw that in simpler brains, in schizophrenia, or in dreams, such ability might be diminished. Viewed in this way, mind might be the personalization of the physical brain as it develops and adapts throughout life. More complex brains, as we saw in Chapter 4, would have more chance for a more individual, less stereotyped mind.

We seem to have returned to the same idea, that of a continuum, already considered for consciousness. If mind is seen as the evolving personal aspect of the physical brain, then how might it relate to consciousness? My particular view is that mind can only be realized when we are conscious. After all, we lose consciousness when we sleep, but we do not lose our mind. However, mind is meaningless if we are unconscious. Hence, consciousness could be seen as the actual firsthand, first-person experience of a certain mind, a personalized brain. Consciousness brings the mind alive; it is the ultimate puzzle to the neuroscientist. It is your most private place.

This ultimate puzzle, the subjective experience of consciousness, is perhaps a good place for any purely scientific survey, namely one of objective facts, to cease. Although all these issues may currently appear daunting, neuroscientists have made exciting and fundamental discoveries, some of which I have tried to review in this book. Slowly, we are seeing the type of questions we must ask and having an idea of the type of answers we should expect. We have seen astounding progress, even since the 1970s, but the adventure is only really just beginning.

FURTHER READING

Blakemore, C. B., and S. A. Greenfield. *Mindwaves: Thoughts on Intelligence, Identity and Consciousness* (Oxford: Basil Blackwell, 1987).

Bloom, F. E., and A. Lazerson. *Brain, Mind, and Behavior* (New York: W. H. Freeman and Co., 1988).

Churchland, P. S., and T. J. Sejnowski. *The Computational Brain* (Cambridge: MIT Press, 1992).

Corsi, P. (ed.). *The Enchanted Loom* (Oxford: Oxford University Press, 1991).

Crick, F. *The Astonishing Hypothesis: The Scientific Search for the Soul* (New York: Macmillan Publishing Co., 1994).

Goldstein, A. *Addiction: From Biology to Drug Policy* (New York: W. H. Freeman and Co., 1994).

Greenfield, S. A. *Journey to the Centers of the Mind: Toward a Science of Consciousness* (New York: W. H. Freeman & Co., 1995).

Kolb, B., and I. Q. Whishaw. *Fundamentals of Human Psychology*, 3rd ed. (New York: W. H. Freeman and Co., 1990).

Levitan, I. B., and L. K. Kazmarek. *The Neuron: Cell and Molecular Biology* (New York: Oxford University Press, 1991).

Oswald, S. *Principles of Cellular, Molecular, and Developmental Neuroscience* (New York: Springer-Verlag, 1989).

Pinel, J. P. J. *Biopsychology*, 2nd ed. (Boston: Allyn and Bacon, 1993).

Rose, S. *The Making of Memory: From Molecules to Mind* (London: Bantam Press, 1992).

Scott, A. *Stairway to the Mind* (New York: Springer-Verlag, 1995).

Shepherd, G. S. *Neurobiology* (Oxford: Oxford University Press, 1983).

Smith, J. *Senses and Sensibilities* (New York: John Wiley and Sons, Inc., 1989).

Zeki, S. *A Vision of the Brain* (Oxford: Blackwell Scientific, 1993).

FROM THE SCIENTIFIC AMERICAN LIBRARY SERIES
....

Barondes, S. H. *Molecules and Mental Illness* (1993).

Hobson, J. A. *Sleep* (1989).

Posner, M. I., and M. E. Raichle. *Images of Mind* (1994).

Ricklefs, R. E., and C. E. Finch. *Aging: A Natural History* (1995).

Snyder, S. *Drugs and the Brain* (1986).

Page numbers in **boldface** refer to illustrations.